When God Doesn't Answer Your Prayer is simple and deep and unflinchingly honest. Jerry brings to the task all his strengths as scholar, pastor and theologian, but bears it to us as poet, pilgrim, storyteller and, especially, man of prayer. Best of all, because he is a man of sorrows himself, Jerry avoids at every turn clichés, smug sanctities, cheap slogans, and instead shapes this whole epistle into one long aching purifying prayer. For those who have ever asked for a meditation on prayer that refuses to woo falsely or promise glibly, but instead deals face-to-face with prayer's earthy messy reality, take heart—your prayer has been answered.

MARK BUCHANAN, Author of *Your God is Too Safe: Rediscovering the Wonder of a God You Can't Control*

When God Doesn't Answer Your Prayer is not just another book on prayer. Jerry Sittser courageously raises the questions most writers conveniently ignore, while he is painfully honest with the heart-wrenching truth mined from his own life. He's an engaging guide with an insightful mind who dares to question our questions while upholding the glory of God. I can't count the number of books I've read on prayer, yet Jerry reveals a side of God and perspectives on prayer that were new to me. Far from mere theory, this book is painfully personal and honest, and it led me to my knees in a new and fresh way. *When God Doesn't Answer Your Prayer* should become standard reading for anyone who seriously desires to explore the problem, and glory, of prayer.

GARY THOMAS, Author of *Sacred Marriage* and *Authentic Faith*

The lessons that Jerry Sittser shares here are ones that he has learned in the deep places, in times of profound spiritual despair. This is a book for everyone who has ever wanted to argue with God about unanswered prayer. I know of no better guide to honest praying.

RICHARD J. MOUW, President, Fuller Theological Seminary

Jerry Sittser dares to ask the tough question of our age—then dares to deliver the even tougher answers.

PATRICIA RAYBON, author of *My First White Friend*

Also by Jerry Sittser
A Grace Disguised
Discovering God's Will

WHEN GOD
DOESN'T ANSWER
YOUR PRAYER

JERRY SITTSER

ZONDERVAN™

GRAND RAPIDS, MICHIGAN 49530 USA

ZONDERVAN™

When God Doesn't Answer Your Prayer
Copyright © 2003 by Gerald L. Sittser

This title is also available as a Zondervan audio product.
Visit www.zondervan.com/audiopages for more information.

Requests for information should be addressed to:

Zondervan, *Grand Rapids, Michigan 49530*

Library of Congress Cataloging-in-Publication Data

Sittser, Gerald Lawson, 1950–.
    When God doesn't answer your prayer / Jerry Sittser.—1ˢᵗ ed.
        p. cm.
    ISBN 0-310-24326-2
    1. Prayer—Christianity. I. Title.
BV220.S67 2004
248.3'2—dc22   2003018880
                                                               CIP

This edition printed on acid-free paper.

All Scripture quotations, unless otherwise indicated, are taken from the *Holy Bible: New International Version*®. NIV®. Copyright © 1973, 1978, 1984 by International Bible Society, or from the *Holy Bible: Today's New International Version*™. Copyright © 2001 by International Bible Society. Used by permission of Zondervan. All rights reserved.

Published in association with the literary agency of Ann Spangler and Company, 1420 Pontiac Road S.E., Grand Rapids, MI 49506.

Interior design by Beth Shagene

Printed in the United States of America

---

03 04 05 06 07 08 09 /❖ DC/ 10 9 8 7 6 5 4 3 2 1

In Memory of Diana Jane Sittser,
who taught me so much about prayer,
through her life and through her death.

CONTENTS

ACKNOWLEDGMENTS

It didn't occur to me until I was almost finished writing this book that my struggle with prayer, my understanding of prayer, and my deep commitment to prayer all came from the same source—my experience as a single father, a role which was thrust upon me suddenly eleven years ago.

I began to think about unanswered prayer after I lost a daughter, Diana Jane; and I committed myself to persist in prayer, in spite of my doubts and confusion, because I had three children left to rear. I wrestled with God, argued with God, pleaded with God, waited upon God, put my requests before God—*prayed*, in other words— because I had lost one child and wanted the best for the other three. Fatherhood has taught me more about prayer than anything else.

Friends, colleagues, and editors have helped to make this book better than it otherwise would have been. Members of the religion department at Whitworth College—Jim Edwards, Terry McGonigal, Roger Mohrlang, and Keith Beebe—read an early draft and met with me for an evening to discuss its strengths and weaknesses. They share my relief that the final draft is much better than the first. Terry McGonigal, the dean of the chapel at Whitworth, also enlisted a dozen students to read an early draft and then a revised draft. Their comments were helpful, too.

Terry Mitchell, Julie Pyle, Ted Ketchum, Kari Neff, Judy Lang, and Greg Orwig read the manuscript and spent an evening at my home discussing it in depth. That evening with them reminded me of the richness of my community in Spokane. Andrea Palpant, former nanny to my children, challenged me to probe the mystery of prayer after she read a draft. Fellow scholars Pam Corpron Parker, Marcia Everett, and Bill Mounce also read a draft and wrote thorough critiques. Christy Lang, a former student, challenged me to reconsider the theological nuances of chapter 4. These friends challenged me to make my prose simpler and my ideas clearer. Donna VanderGriend encouraged me to press on and reminded me that I was capable of writing something worth reading. My sister and brother-in-law, Diane and Jack Veltkamp, raised good questions about the manuscript along the way, too.

Three students, David Webster, Gabe Schmidt, and Adam Cleaveland, provided valuable assistance. David spent many hours helping with the research; Gabe typed footnotes; and Adam searched for and found some excellent quotes that appear at the beginning of several chapters.

The people whose stories appear in the book were kind enough to give me permission to tell their stories to the larger public. I appreciate their willingness to let me write about their experiences and to let others learn from their suffering. We are richer and wiser because of their generosity.

My agent, Ann Spangler, who has become a dear friend over the years, landed the contract with Zondervan and served as a creative consultant, critic, and sounding board. My editor, Sandra Vander-Zicht, encouraged me from start to finish, communicated grace to me when I most needed it, and expected the best from me. Her instincts for good writing never cease to amaze me. I only wish I could rise to her level of expertise. Verlyn Verbrugge, another editor at Zondervan, touched up the manuscript and made several helpful suggestions. John Topliff and the marketing team at Zondervan have invested in my success as a writer over the past few years, too. This book is the third that I have published with Zondervan. I am grateful for the investment they have made in me.

I carry Diana Jane in my heart. She is at the heart of this book and never far from my mind. I dedicate it to her memory.

PROLOGUE

The greatest tragedy of life is not unanswered prayer,
but unoffered prayer.
F. B. Meyer

I HAVE ALWAYS BEEN DRAWN TO THE DIFFICULT QUESTIONS OF THE Christian faith—for example, *Why do we suffer?* and *How can we discover the will of God when the future seems so unclear?* But for me perhaps the most troubling question of all is, *Why doesn't God answer our prayers?* The question is a vexation to me because prayer is the one discipline in the Christian faith that makes us feel entirely dependent on God and thus sets us up for profound disappointment when God doesn't respond to our needs and requests.

I have pondered this question deeply and for a long time, but never more so than after our family suffered a terrible tragedy in 1991. The question of unanswered prayer suddenly became a life-and-death matter to me. I realized then that how I answered this question would set the course of my spiritual journey for years to come.

This question is on the minds of most praying people, though they rarely admit it because it seems so irreverent, like cursing during Holy Communion. Still, it's an important question. In one sense, it's *the* question. We often turn to God at our most vulnerable moments, when all seems lost unless God steps in. Why does God remain distant, silent, and hard when we call on him? If God doesn't respond when we need him most, then why pray at all?

I am not talking here about silly and superficial prayers that go unanswered, prayers that we would probably not dare to say if we thought twice about it. I have uttered many of those prayers over the years. I have sat in the bleachers of basketball games and prayed for victory when the game seemed lost; I have asked that lights turn green when I was in a hurry; I have pleaded that a stomachache pass after I gorged myself on too much food. It is silly to complain when God doesn't answer these trivial prayers.

But sometimes we pray for something that really counts, to us and presumably to God—the conversion of a neighbor, deliverance from alcoholism, guidance for the future, the healing of a sick child, food for a starving people. We pray with sincerity, faith, and conviction, as if our life depended on it—which, of course, it probably does. We ask God for something that seems so right and true. What should we do if God doesn't come through in circumstances that make us desperate for his intervention? It is hard to accept when God seems to ignore our best prayers, and harder still to keep praying.

If I have a favorite character in the Bible, it's the apostle Peter. He was a spiritual swashbuckler, the most intrepid of Jesus' disciples. Bold and brash, he took risks, signed up, and jumped in, but he also blundered and bumbled a lot. He was Jesus' closest friend and biggest problem.

This book will have a little of Peter's personality in it. I can't tackle this troublesome question with dispassionate objectivity, as if I were conducting a scientific experiment about something that doesn't matter to me or to anyone else. However thoughtful and objective I try to be, I will struggle on these pages, too. I have no choice in the matter because the topic is too important to me.

A typical Jew in his day, Peter knew his Psalms. I wonder how Psalm 131 influenced him. I can only guess that it affected him deeply as he pondered the mysteries of his faith and matured as a believer.

O LORD, my heart is not lifted up,
my eyes are not raised too high;
I do not occupy myself with things
too great and too marvelous for me.
But I have calmed and quieted my soul,
like a weaned child with its mother;
my soul is like a weaned child that is with me.
O Israel, hope in the LORD
from this time on and forevermore.[1]

Psalm 131 reminds us that when we wrestle with difficult questions, we should recognize our limitations. There is much we can learn; there is much, however, that will remain hidden from us. Perhaps the question *Why doesn't God answer our prayers?* is not even the best question to ask because there might not be a simple, convenient, and obvious answer. It might be too mysterious and lofty to us. Perhaps *how we respond* in the face of such mystery is more important than whether or not we will ever find an answer to the question itself.

The problem of unanswered prayer touches on a sensitive area, as if scratching a wound that refuses to heal. In several public settings over the past year or two I have asked a series of questions to discover the depth and breadth of concern over this issue. "How many here have prayed prayers that were not answered?" I have asked. The vast majority of people always raise their hands. "How many of you would say that these prayers were serious and sincere, worthy of being answered?" I ask. Again, the vast majority of people raise their hands. "How many would say that these unanswered prayers precipitated a spiritual crisis in your lives?" Not surprisingly, most people raise their hands a third time.

It is risky to take this problem on. I feel as if I am standing on the edge of the Grand Canyon, staring into the abyss below. I am filled with both terror and wonder. I want to back away toward safety but remain frozen to the spot. I find myself compelled to ask hard questions about unanswered prayer because everything in me wants an answer and needs an answer. Still, I realize that the answer itself poses a threat. On the one hand, it might turn me away from God and undermine my desire to pray. On the other hand, it also might draw me deeper into God and engender in me even greater passion to pray.

I find that I am not alone. Most people I know have the same questions, feel the same vexation, and stand on the edge of the same abyss. If you are one of those people, I invite you to join me as we explore this mystery together.

CHAPTER 1

ARE YOU
LISTENING, GOD?

*If many remedies are prescribed
for an illness, you can be certain
that the illness has no cure.*
A. P. CHEKHOV, FROM *THE CHERRY ORCHARD*

ELEVEN YEARS AGO I LOST MY FOUR-YEAR-OLD DAUGHTER, DIANA Jane, in a car accident that also took the lives of my wife, Lynda, and my mother, Grace. Their deaths, so sudden and brutal, set me on a spiritual journey that has continued to this day. The journey has been both grueling and wonderful, and the landscape I have crossed in the intervening years has been both bleak and beautiful. I have traveled through deserts that seemed as stark and dead as the moon; I have traveled through meadows lush with wildflowers. I have pondered more questions than I could name and number. But one question has remained, even after all these years: It is the question of unanswered prayer.

I prayed for my daughter's protection on the morning of the accident, as I had every morning since her birth. But something went desperately wrong that day. My prayer for Diana Jane was not answered, or so it seemed at the time.

When our kids were young, Lynda and I followed a bedtime ritual as predictable as the seasons. We never dared deviate from it. If we tried, our kids would resist us like sailors leading a mutiny. We put them in the bath first, usually alone, though sometimes in pairs. Then we dried them off, dressed them in their jammies, and sent them off to bed, where we cuddled, read stories, and sang songs. Finally, just before turning the lights out, we prayed. More often than not they fell asleep right away, with the exception of Diana Jane, who became a master at finding excuses to prolong the ritual as long as she could.

We taught them *how* to pray, too. We started simple, using a centuries-old prayer known the world over.

> *Now I lay me down to sleep;*
> *I pray thee, Lord, my soul to keep.*
> *If I should die before I wake,*
> *I pray thee, Lord, my soul to take.*

This prayer reflects a concern that we in the Western world have largely outgrown. Before the advent of vaccines, penicillin, and surgery, many children died from disease, like weak animals culled from the herd before they could reach adulthood. Most deaths occurred during the night. Parents feared a visitation from the grim reaper, who would come under the shadow of darkness to snuff out the life of a precious child.

Lynda and I not only prayed *with* the kids, but we also prayed *for* them. I always prayed for them early in the morning, as I still do. I would stumble into the kitchen and make a pot of coffee. While the coffee brewed, I would peek at the paper. Then, after pouring myself a cup of coffee, I would sit down in a special chair and pray.

Some of my prayers were token and halfhearted, uttered more out of habit than in genuine faith. But not when I prayed for my kids. Lynda and I weren't supposed to have our own kids in the first place. That we had four children in six years was so miraculous to us that it engendered a deep sense of gratitude and responsibility in me. I never felt comfortable and adequate in the role of father. I was afraid I would mess up the kids. So I tried to follow Lynda's example, sought advice from experienced fathers, and prayed.

Oh, how I prayed for my kids! Praying for them was like breathing. I prayed because I loved them deeply and wanted to raise them well. I prayed that my kids would grow in faith, mature in character, discover their life's calling, build good friendships, and serve human needs. I prayed God's blessing on them. Finally, I prayed for their protection. I did not qualify my prayers. There were no "if God wills." I wanted them kept safe and secure, healthy and strong. I wanted to see them grow up to honor Jesus. I wanted them to outlive me.

If Diana Jane were alive today, she would be fifteen, a sophomore in high school. She hardly seems real to me now, though I still catch glimpses of her in my imagination. Unlike Lynda, who has remained in my memory pretty much as she was before she died, Diana Jane has changed because she would be so different now were she still alive.

I try to picture her as a teenager. She was always winning and wild, like a pet that could never quite be tamed. She was quick to flash a mischievous smile, walk on her tiptoes, and tease her siblings. She either giggled or cried, with nothing in between. She would press us to the limit, but with such a sweet disposition that we usually ended up laughing. I wonder what she would be like now—her height and appearance, her talents and interests, her personality and tastes. What flavor of ice cream would she like? How would she wear her hair? Who would be her best friend? What would be her favorite books and movies?

We were all together when the accident occurred. Three died, four survived—my daughter, Catherine, my two sons, David and John, and me. The scene of the accident was chaotic and apocalyptic, like something out of a disaster movie. We had to wait almost an hour before an emergency vehicle transported us to the nearest hospital, which was another hour away. The four of us drove in virtual silence, as if we were sitting inside a great cathedral, struck dumb by its grandeur. It gave me time—it actually felt more like an eternity—to think.

I realized in that moment that there was nothing I could do to reverse the catastrophe that had just devastated our family. Still, like a doctor in an emergency room taking extraordinary measures to stop the bleeding, I wanted to control the damage. I looked at my three traumatized children and decided then and there to do whatever would be required to help them through the crisis. My commitment to them from that point on became as fierce as a wounded animal trying to protect its young. I prayed for them, too, right there in the sad and holy silence of that emergency vehicle.

But a few days later a question arose in the back of my mind. That question nagged at me like a mild headache that refuses to go away, no matter how much pain killer you take. Why are you praying, Jerry? You prayed for Diana Jane's protection the morning of the accident, and look what happened! Why didn't God answer that prayer? Can you take prayer seriously, ever again?

Why Unanswered Prayer?

In the years that followed, I realized that it's not just my question. It's most everyone's. Why doesn't God answer our prayers? Not the silly and trivial prayers we say sometimes when we're in a pinch but the sincere prayers we say when we're in desperate need.

It is no longer an abstract question to me, the kind of question that some philosophy class might explore. It's a real question, as gritty and gutsy as the painful experience that forced me to ask it. I simply couldn't keep praying without finding an answer to it.

It wouldn't be such a serious question if we didn't take prayer so seriously. That we pray almost goes without saying, no matter what the circumstances. A grandparent says a prayer of thanksgiving at a holiday celebration. A military chaplain prays for the safety of a special military unit before it launches a secret mission. A parent cries out to God in anguish at the bedside of a sick child.

Prayer is partly a habit. As a habit, prayer is something we learn to do and have to work at, especially when we don't feel like it. Some of us succeed, becoming proficient and consistent, which are the fruits of effort and discipline; others of us fail, lacking the motivation to pray day in and day out. But prayer is also a reflex, like the jerk of a leg when the doctor's mallet strikes it or the blink of the eyes when a loud noise goes off. As a reflex prayer seems to run deep in human nature, as if we have no choice in the matter. Facing danger or difficulty, opportunity or challenge, we feel compelled to pray, even if we're not sure there is a God out there to whom we are praying.

> *Facing danger or difficulty, opportunity or challenge, we feel compelled to pray, even if we're not sure there is a God out there to whom we are praying.*

Prayer seems to work, too, which only makes the problem of unanswered prayer more bewildering. At least *some* of our prayers are clearly answered, often in astonishing ways. I have witnessed many answers to prayer over the course of the last twenty-five years. I have seen a young man healed of cancer (though his prognosis was like a death sentence hanging over his head); I have watched churches come alive, marriages restored, and mental health problems overcome. We may pray out of habit or as a reflex; but we also pray because we get results—at least some of the time. Some people even use a prayer journal, recording their requests and God's answers. When a recipe produces superb food time and again, we are likely to continue using it.

But what about *unanswered* prayer? What should we do and how should we respond when our prayers—prayers that seem right and true and good—go unanswered, even when we say them with reverence, believing that they reflect what God really wants for us? Unanswered prayer is like a raw nerve in the Christian community. We pray because we believe in God. We tell God our needs—healing, restoration, protection, guidance, wisdom—but God doesn't give us what we need. Sometimes God seems as cold and distant as some far-off galaxy.

I know the conventional answer. It goes like this: God answers *every* prayer. He says "yes" to some prayers and "no" to others. There is something tidy and cogent about this answer. It provides an easy and rational answer to a troubling question. But sometimes personal experience makes this answer hard to accept. The formula doesn't pass the test. I can understand why God says "no" to some prayers, but not to all. What about a distraught couple who has just lost a son to cancer, though they prayed for healing? Or missionaries who have labored for years in a mission that was shut down because of lack of results, though they asked God for conversions? Or a group of high school kids who lost a good friend to suicide, though they asked God to deliver him from his emotional affliction?

Did God simply decide to say "no"? It seems hard to believe.

THE RAW NERVE

Bob Mitchell, former president of Young Life and former vice president of World Vision, preached a sermon in our church recently in which he quoted from a letter he received almost fifty years ago, in May of 1955. The letter was written by Jim Elliot, who had recently moved to Ecuador, with his young wife and baby daughter, to pioneer a new missionary outreach to the Auca Indians. The Aucas lived in a remote area and were considered hostile to outsiders.

Elliot expressed gladness that "the gospel is creeping a little farther out into this big no-man's land of Amazonia." He also mentioned a mutual friend and partner in the missionary endeavor, Ed, who had already left to make contact with the tribe. Expressing both excitement and foreboding, Elliot charged Bob Mitchell to pray for them, especially for Ed. "There are rumors that the same tribe is scouting around there now, so don't forget to pray for Ed—that the

Lord will keep him alive as well as make him effective in declaring the truth about Christ."

Of course Bob did not forget to pray for these courageous friends. He prayed for their protection and for the success of their work. He was only one of hundreds who prayed for this new mission. But several months later those friends—Ed, Jim, and three others—were murdered by members of the very tribe they were trying to reach. Bob's prayer was not answered.

Nor are many others. The same story keeps repeating itself. It just involves different people, occurs under different circumstances, and leads to a different disappointment.

Take Pete and Shirley. In their sixties, they were nearing retirement after forty years of faithful service to the church. He was a pastor, she his supporter and an energetic volunteer. Their last church was their best. Though a large congregation (over 1,400 in attendance on a typical Sunday), it had become like a family to them. God had prospered their ministry at the church, too. The church was healthy and vibrant. It was a lighthouse in the community, a place that was attracting broken people.

Then the criticism started. A few in leadership began to question the pastor's vision and the church's lack of explosive growth. One leader said, "This church was once the flagship of the denomination. I want it to return to that position of glory once again." He even threatened them. "You have six months to turn things around, or you're out!"

Pete and Shirley were shocked. They thought that the board understood their philosophy—grow the church in faith, love, and service, and it will eventually grow in numbers, too. They tried to explain their vision and its biblical foundation; they emphasized the importance of availability, brokenness, and confession.

But the criticism continued. Most members of the church were supportive. Many cared for them, prayed for them, and encouraged them, especially during the conflict. Some remained distant and silent. But a small group of people launched a campaign against them. People betrayed them and made false accusations against them. The church became divided, a hostile place, a cancerous community.

They cried out to God. They prayed constantly and asked others to do the same. They fasted and claimed the promises of God. They begged for protection, vindication, and deliverance. "We remembered the deliverance of Joseph from prison, David before Goliath, Elijah on Mount Carmel, Daniel in the lion's den, Peter in prison. Our God was the same God. He would fight for us."

But it became clear after a long battle that there would be no reconciliation and peace. So they resigned. Their farewell was like a funeral. Their losses overwhelmed them—community, friendships, financial security, reputation.

What surprised and bewildered them most of all, however, was God's silence. "God did not answer our prayers. Heaven was strangely silent, cold, distant, as if made of brass. It felt as if we knocked and pounded on the door of heaven until our knuckles were raw and bleeding, and still there was only silence. Why pray when all you get is silence?"

Or take Eddie. Our family met Eddie when we visited Kenya in the summer of 2000 to do volunteer work. Eddie was a refugee. He had not seen or heard from his family in ten years and had no idea if they were still alive. His suffering, however, had ennobled and deepened him. He had become a devout Christian, and he wanted to serve as a pastor in Africa. So he attended a university in Nairobi and was just about to graduate when we met him.

He had big dreams for his future. He thought that the best preparation he could receive for ministry was in the United States. He researched schools, applied for admission, and lined up financial support. He was finally accepted into his school of choice. All seemed ready, except for securing a visa. He brought letters of support, a financial statement, and an endorsement from a thriving evangelical church in Nairobi when he met with embassy officials. He received coaching from someone who works within the government. He did everything short of offering a bribe.

He prayed, too, every step along the way, because he was certain that it was the will of God for him to study in the United States, where he believed that the best education was available. It seemed so clear to him. But the government would not issue him a visa. He tried again, thinking that God was testing his faith. Still no visa. He tried a third time. Again, he came away empty-handed. His prayer was not answered.

How many stories end the same way? We pray for deliverance from an addiction but continue to struggle with the same torment. We pray for guidance but remain directionless. We pray for healing but a loved one dies, though in the prime of her life. We pray for restoration but the marriage ends in a bitter divorce. We pray for justice but fail to see racism and poverty recede. We pray for food but watch helplessly as people die of starvation.

When C. S. Lewis was only nine, his beloved mother became ill with cancer. The doctor performed surgery right in Lewis's home. A half century after the experience Lewis could still describe the sights, sounds, and smells with a terrible vividness. Lewis prayed desperately for her recovery, as only a terrified boy of nine could pray. But it was all in vain. The impact of her death—the loss itself, the change in his father's character, the disruption in his home—left an indelible imprint on Lewis and contributed to his rejection of Christianity, all precipitated by unanswered prayer.[1]

A friend wrote to me recently, after praying with scores of others for the restoration of her marriage (which later ended in divorce), "I know it shook the faith of legions of Christians with carefully held beliefs on who God is and how God operates. I still don't get it. I *really* want to get it. Would it be so difficult to lift the veil and let me in on just a smidgen of that answer?"

It is a wonder that we pray at all, considering how often we have been disappointed by unanswered prayer. As writer and seminary professor Barbara Brown Taylor asks, "Why do any of us keep wishing for things we know won't happen? Why do we keep tossing the coins of our hearts' desires into pools of still water that swallow them up without a sound?"[2]

Easy Answers

After the accident few people tried to mitigate our trauma by explaining why it happened. Still, two stand out. One person said, "It is a terrible loss. But I believe that you have been set aside for some significant mission." To which I wanted to say, "You mean that we didn't have a significant mission *before* the accident?" Another person said, "I guess they were so special to God that he wanted them in heaven with him." To which I wanted to say, "Does that mean that the rest of us are *not* special to God?" These explanations were well-meaning, but not helpful.

There are other convenient answers, too. "Well," we may say to someone who has just lost a loved one, "at least she is in a better place now." That, of course, is probably true, though it doesn't really provide much comfort. If this statement were literally true, then we should probably pray that every one of our Christian friends and family members dies as soon as possible so that they can all go to a better place and be with God in heaven.

"God's ways are higher than our ways," someone says, trivializing a powerful text from the prophet Isaiah, as if the mystery of God's ways makes prayer irrelevant and obsolete.

"I guess your prayers were not in accordance with God's will," another says, which implies that God's will is unknowable to us, having nothing to do with his promises as recorded in the Bible.

"Even God can't reverse the natural course of events," still another says. But God has reversed the natural course of events, as we read in the New Testament. If God did it then, why not now?

In fact, the Bible only exacerbates the problem. It actually sets us up for disappointment by making grandiose promises that God doesn't always keep—or so it would seem. Consider the outrageous promises that Jesus himself makes!

> So I say to you: Ask and it will be given to you; seek and you will find; knock and the door will be opened to you. For everyone who asks receives; those who seek find; and to those who knock, the door will be opened.[3]

> Very truly I tell you, all who have faith in me will do the works I have been doing, and they will do even greater things than these, because I am going to the Father. And I will do whatever you ask in my name, so that the Father may be glorified in the Son. You may ask me for anything in my name, and I will do it.[4]

A simple reading of these texts leads to a simple conclusion: If we pray, God will answer. What then is to be done when God *doesn't* answer our prayers?

Andrew Murray, writer of the classic *With Christ in the School of Prayer,* argued—rightly so—that the promises of God are the foundation for effective praying. We pray not only because God commands us to pray but also because God promises to answer our prayers. We have the assurance of answered prayer from none other than Jesus himself. What God promises, we can and must claim.

But Murray was so sure of Jesus' teaching on this point that he believed unanswered prayer was always due to bad praying and thus always our fault.

> This is the fixed eternal law of the kingdom: if you ask and receive not, it must be because there is something amiss or wanting in the prayer. Hold on; let the Word and Spirit teach you to pray aright, but do not let go the confidence He seeks to waken: Everyone who asketh, receiveth.[5]

As Murray noted, Jesus awakens an expectation that our prayers will be answered. But what happens if our prayers are not answered? Does it always mean that we don't have enough faith, that we have somehow prayed wrongly, or that we are simply unworthy of answers to prayer?

Why doesn't God answer our prayers? What, if anything, can we do about it?

OUR PROBLEM?

I have pondered possible answers for a long time. I think such answers come down to the following ones. First, perhaps there is something wrong with our motives. We could be praying as hypocrites—harboring a grudge, committing a willful sin, making frivolous requests, or praying selfishly. In other words, we could be like an employee who politely asks his boss for a raise, though the boss knows that this employee has been slandering him for months. Unanswered prayer can be our own fault, as we all know. We could be praying in an unworthy manner. Unanswered prayer invites us to take a hard and close look at ourselves, which often exposes the unseemly side of our spiritual life that most people never see, like worms and grubs that hide underneath decorative rocks in a garden.

Second, something could be wrong with our faith. It could be that we have just enough faith to pray, daring to ask God for something that is important to us, but not quite enough to receive answers to prayer. We could be praying with too much doubt in our hearts. For example, we ask God for money that we desperately need—say, to buy food for our kids or to pay overdue medical bills—but we lack confidence that God will answer that prayer. A seed of doubt takes root in the soul like a weed that keeps coming back, no matter how hard we try to stomp it out. We know we're not praying with absolute sincerity, either because we don't believe that God will answer our prayers or because we don't think we're worthy of it.

Third, something could be wrong with the way we say our prayers. We aren't using the right words, following the right formula, making the right requests, speaking with enough forcefulness. American culture is obsessed with techniques. We think that once we master the right technique, the world is ours for the taking. We spend billions of dollars a year on books, tapes, and seminars that teach us those techniques. Sometimes we approach prayer in the same way. If we know what to say and how to say it, then we will receive.

During the Ming Dynasty the emperor of China built the Temple of Heaven to pray for the prosperity of his kingdom. When he stood on a particular stone and prayed toward heaven, his voice would echo back to him as if he had been shouting, though anyone standing next to him would hear only a whisper. Tradition says that heaven could hear the emperor best in that particular place. Is that how prayer works?

These explanations have merit; a grain of truth lies in all of them. Purity of motive is important and necessary. So is faith. So are the right words. I won't dispute any of this. Yet these explanations leave me cold, too, because I think they force needless introspection and lead to self-punishment. Does God only answer the prayers of perfect people, perfectly pronounced, uttered in perfect faith?

Imagine a teenager growing up in a conflicted home. Her parents fight all the time. She tries her best to avoid her dad; she clashes with her mom. She is angry at both of them. She is sick of her dad's passivity and her mother's mercurial temper. Every night she prays that her mom and dad will get along, but nothing seems to change. She knows that her motives aren't pure, her faith isn't perfect, her prayers aren't polished, precise, and articulate. Is that why her prayers aren't being answered?

It would be convenient, I suppose, to explain away every incident of unanswered prayer as the fault of the people who did the praying. At least there would be a rational explanation of the problem: We are to blame, every time. But doesn't this answer contradict the reason why we pray? We pray as fragile, broken people. It would strike me as impossibly demanding if we had to prove ourselves worthy of answered prayer by stellar performance, precise articulation, and unwavering faith. Prayer seems truer to me when it spits and mutters and cries.

> *Prayer seems truer to me when it spits and mutters and cries.*

Prayer turns away from self, however worthy or unworthy, and seeks God, asking him for mercy. When we approach God, we have nothing to use as capital, no commodities that we can trade, no sum of righteousness that we can use to buy answers to prayer. The thief on the cross did not have to complete a rehabilitation program before Jesus would say, "Today you will be with me in paradise."

GOD'S PROBLEM?

But there's still one more possible answer to the question, one that I find far more unsettling. The problem could be God's. What does unanswered prayer say about the character of God? Jesus taught that God is like a father who cares for us and wants to meet our needs. If God is, as Jesus said, a loving Father, why doesn't he answer our prayers? Aren't fathers supposed to meet the genuine needs of their children and respond with generosity when their children ask for good things? Unanswered prayer makes God seem distant, remote, and uncaring, more like an abusive boss than like a loving father. Unanswered prayer seems to raise questions about whether God truly loves us.

Like many authors who have written books about prayer, Harry Emerson Fosdick, the famous pastor of the historic Riverside Church in New York City in the early twentieth century, suggested that prayer is meaningful only to the degree that it is rooted in the character of God. "For prayer at least, a God who does not care, does not count."[6] But how do we know God cares? Surely we see God's character manifested in the biblical story of Jesus. But we also experience his character when we pray. What does unanswered prayer say about the character of God?

As I have explored the question of why God doesn't answer my own prayers, I have wondered whether it is possible to find an answer at all. Perhaps God simply chooses, for reasons known only to him, *not* to answer our prayers, however worthy we think our prayers are. He may do so for reasons that are and will remain a mystery to us.

But what kind of answer is that? If we will never know why God doesn't answer our prayers, we'll never learn how to pray with greater confidence and conviction, or even dare to pray at all. We will be left shaking our heads, mystified by God's elusiveness. The motivation to pray will drain out of us as if our souls had a leak. We'll finally give up trying, stop praying, and surrender to fate.

It seems that any way you cut it, the problem remains.

My mind wanders back to the morning of September 27, 1991. I have turned that morning over in my mind a thousand times. I try to remember what exactly I prayed that day and how I prayed it. I wonder if I used the wrong words or prayed in an unworthy manner. Was I too frivolous, too confident, or too casual? Did I lack faith and sincerity? I think about God, too. What happened to him that day? Where was he? Was God as surprised by the accident as I was? Or did God have the accident planned, as if following a script he had written before the world began?

What happened that day? Why didn't God answer my prayer?

QUESTIONS FOR DISCUSSION

1. Think of a time or two when God didn't answer your prayer. What happened as a result? How did you feel?

2. What do you make of all the promises in the Bible concerning prayer?

3. Why doesn't God answer all our prayers? What possibilities are expressed in this chapter?

4. Whose problem is unanswered prayer? Ours? God's? Is there another explanation?

CHAPTER 2

THE TRUE HEART
OF PRAYER

We may pray most when we say least,
and we may pray least when we say most.
ST. AUGUSTINE OF HIPPO

I PRAY MOST OF THE TIME IN ARMCHAIR SECURITY. MY PRAYERS ARE sincere but not desperate, at least not as they were in the months following the accident, when I *had* to pray, even though I sometimes doubted the God to whom I was praying. Now my circumstances are so favorable that I'm not sure I really need answers to prayer. Of course it would be nice if God did answer my prayers, just as it would be nice if I could trade in my 1991 Voyager for a BMW convertible.

The relative comfort and prosperity of my life takes the edge off my prayers. I say them, but I don't always cry them. I feel disappointment when my prayers go unanswered, to be sure, but it hardly precipitates a crisis. Why should it? I don't have that much to lose if my prayers aren't answered. Consequently, I can become as complacent and casual in my praying as someone ordering dessert at a restaurant after having eaten a big dinner. Deprived of dessert, I will leave the restaurant with a full belly anyway. Deprived of answers to prayer, I will survive all the same.

Not that prayers uttered in these kinds of circumstances are wrong or unworthy. That my life is now comfortable and secure is not my own doing but a tribute to the goodness of God. Prayers of gratitude demonstrate our awareness that the bounty of our lives is the result of God's generosity. But such bounty can also lure us into complacency and self-satisfaction.

> *When all other courses of action have been eliminated, when we stand at the edge of the abyss, when we approach God with empty hands and an aching heart, then we draw close to the true heart of prayer.*

Unanswered prayer never becomes a significant issue until we really *need* an answer to prayer, until our life depends on an answer. Then we cry out to God out of a deep sense of need. We pray out of desperation. When all other courses of action have been eliminated, when we stand at the edge of the abyss, when we approach God with empty hands and an aching heart, then we draw close to the true heart of prayer. But we also become all the more vulnerable to the crushing disappointment of unanswered prayer.

Desperation drives us to prayer; desperation can also drive us to despair if our prayers go unanswered.

OUR DESPERATE NEED FOR GOD

I met Kevin just a few months ago. He looked like a man who had recently recovered from a serious illness. He was tall and very thin, sporting a trimmed beard and wearing jeans and a flannel shirt. We were serving at The City Gate, a storefront church in downtown Spokane that reaches out to the poor, the homeless, ex-inmates, street kids, alcoholics, and addicts. It is part church, part soup kitchen, part clinic, part food pantry, and part drop-in center.

We had just finished serving dinner to the hundred and fifty or so people who showed up for the weekly Wednesday evening meal of spaghetti, French bread, salad, peaches, and cake. Perhaps thirty people lingered, sitting around the tables for conversation, a second cup of coffee, or a game of cards.

I introduced myself.

"Hi. I'm Jerry. I come most Wednesday nights. I haven't seen you before. You new here?"

"Yeah, just came to Spokane. I'm Kevin. Nice to meet you."

We shook hands.

"How'd you find out about The City Gate?"

"Some people I met earlier this week told me about it. So I came. Now here I am, serving already. I guess they needed the help."

"So what do you do? I mean, for a living."

"Right now I'm unemployed."

"Where are you living?"

"I'm sleeping on a friend's living room sofa until I get my own place. I just met him last week. It keeps me off the streets."

"Do you have family here?"

"Not really. I have two kids, but I haven't seen them for a while. One lives in Portland, the other is in jail."

An uncomfortable silence followed. I felt heat rise in my face, the first flush of embarrassment. I wanted to steer the conversation in another direction. But I had run out of questions. I had done it again, broken one of the cardinal rules of the ministry. You don't ask stupid middle-class questions at The City Gate.

Then Kevin looked at me and, as if to pardon my stupidity through an act of pure generosity, said, "I was a heroin addict for seventeen years. I lost everything—my job, my family, my health. I just got out of treatment. Jesus helped me kick the habit. I don't know what I would do without Jesus."

Suddenly everything had changed. I was no longer the heroic outsider who visits The City Gate once a week to serve the "less fortunate," as we like to call them. I was standing in the presence of a saint who knew that without Jesus he would probably be dead.

In that moment I realized why I go to The City Gate. My motives are decidedly mixed. I volunteer there as much for myself as for the people this storefront church serves. I used to think, "There by the grace of God go I." Not any more. Now I think, "There by the grace of God I should be"—in that place, with those people, on the margins.

I forget all too quickly how much I need Jesus, how much we all need Jesus. When I'm at The City Gate, I see with greater clarity what I know to be true in my head but not always in my heart—why Jesus came, whom Jesus spent time with, how much Jesus loved the needy. I don't envy their circumstances, but I do envy their awareness—raw, constant, and deep—of their need for God's grace. My life is so padded with wealth and privilege and success that I run the risk of becoming dull to God, too "spoiled by God's indulgence," as John Calvin put it.[1] The City Gate reminds me of how much I depend on God, even when I don't realize it. I enjoy many of God's earthly gifts, but I tend to ignore the giver. Ironically, his gifts keep me from seeing my desperate need for him.

As I look back over the many years I have prayed, I see a common theme. In many cases I prayed only when I really had to, when hard times forced me to. I was desperate for something; I knew I needed God's intervention, God's help, God's grace. I prayed when starting a new job because I felt inadequate. I prayed when a loved one was sick because I felt helpless. I prayed when there were problems in our home, like the constant bickering between Catherine and David, that defied a simple solution. I prayed when missionary friends on the field faced a crisis in the church they were serving. And I prayed—oh, how I prayed!—that God would restore order, equilibrium, and wholeness to my family after the accident.

THE PHARISEE AND THE TAX COLLECTOR

Jesus told a story to challenge those "who were confident of their own righteousness and looked down on everyone else."[2] Typical for Jesus, he takes what was a common occurrence in his day to set the scene for his story and to challenge conventional wisdom.

His story contains only two characters—one a Pharisee, the other a tax collector. They both entered the temple to pray. The Pharisee marched boldly to the front of the temple and told God all the reasons why he was better than everyone else. He listed his religious accomplishments, as if God was lucky to have him on his side. Then, full of self-satisfaction, he ended his prayer and left the temple. The tax collector, by contrast, stayed in the back of the temple. He didn't dare raise his eyes toward heaven. Beating his breast, he muttered, "God, have mercy on me, a sinner."[3]

The Pharisees were upright citizens and leaders in the community, like pastors or physicians in our society. They embodied all that was right and noble and true in Judaism, and they were deeply committed to serving God in their daily lives, largely by obeying the Torah. They wanted to be "set apart"—the basic meaning of the word *Pharisee*—in order to resist the encroachment of the ungodly world. The Roman Empire's occupation of Israel engendered a great deal of resentment. The Pharisees opposed the occupation and strove to preserve the Jewish faith. Popular in their day, they attracted a wide following, though not many people could live according to their rigorous standards.

Tax collectors, however, carried a bad reputation, and a well deserved one, too. Rome was a massive foreign power, and Roman soldiers could be brutal. Most Jews detested Rome. One of the most obvious reasons for this hatred was the Roman practice of taxation. Jews paid exorbitant taxes to Rome. Someone had to collect those taxes. That odious duty was handed over to a handful of Jewish traitors who worked for Rome and fleeced their own people. These

Jewish tax collectors became very rich, but were also unpopular. Their closest counterpart in our culture would be a pimp or a drug dealer.

PRIDEFUL PRAYING

Jesus' story in Luke 18 does not condemn the Pharisee for how he lived any more than it commends the tax collector for how he lived. What makes the Pharisee bad was his pride and contempt. He looked down at people whom he considered his inferiors. He despised them for their moral failure and lack of religious piety.

The Pharisee thought he was a godly man because of his good behavior. He had lived a righteous life, done his duty to God and humanity, and excelled in godly behavior. On one level the Pharisee had every reason to be proud of his religious accomplishments. After all, he *had* accomplished what he claimed in his prayer. His performance was impressive. Moreover, he even expressed gratitude to God for his achievements, which demonstrates at least some degree of humility and piety. The problem is, he thought God should be grateful, too—for him.

At his pious best, the Pharisee prayed as if it was Thanksgiving Day. He told God that he was grateful he was not like "bad" people who violated the moral and civil law—thieves, adulterers, murderers, and the like—nor even like the tax collector whom he spotted out of the corner of his eye, whose reputation made him an outsider in Israel. The Pharisee reminded God that he tithed his income and fasted twice a week, behavior that exceeded what was normally expected of religious leaders in his day.

This Pharisee was a respected leader, well educated, active in the synagogue, a pillar of the community. Were he living in our world, he would be the kind who donates to worthy causes, sits on committees, pays his taxes in full, defends the moral order, practices piety as publicly as possible, cares for his family, and keeps his yard immaculate. He would never consider divorcing his wife, watching a questionable movie, or swearing at a referee who had just made a bad call at his son's basketball game, not even under his breath. This man was righteous.

ARE WE PHARISEES?

Suddenly I realize that I am this man. I am the Pharisee. I am to the folks who visit The City Gate what he was to the tax collector, living worlds apart from their kind of desperate need and feeling smugly satisfied that I have made something of my life.

Darrell Guder, a missiologist who teaches at Princeton Seminary, once said that if we want to understand the relevance of the New Testament to our own lives, we should read it as if we belonged to the party of the Pharisees because, if we had lived back then, most of us would have been card-carrying members in good standing. Like them, many of us are successful in life, and we attribute our success to religion.

My faith has certainly worked wonders for me. If I were more entrepreneurial, I would market it and make millions. It has helped me to discipline my appetites, strengthen my friendships, create stability in my life, and serve others. I have accomplished far more than I ever thought I would, and I have received more than my fair share of accolades. Much of the prosperity I enjoy is due to the direct or indirect influence of faith. Moreover, I make sure that I thank God and others as often as I can. I am as pious as they come!

How ironic that the quality of my Christian life tempts me to be proud, to evaluate my work in light of the failures of others, and to celebrate my circumstances in light of the misery of others. Like the Pharisee, I'm grateful that I'm not poor, unemployed, unpopular, and burdened with big problems.

C. S. Lewis suggested that pride causes us to think in comparative and competitive terms. Pride makes us feel superior, whatever the standard of comparison happens to be, thus tempting us to forget about God.

> In God you come up against something which is in every respect immeasurably superior to yourself. Unless you know God as that—and, therefore, know yourself as nothing in comparison—you do not know God at all. As long as you are proud you cannot know God. A proud man is always looking down on things and people: and, of course, as long as you are looking down, you cannot see something that is above you.[4]

We don't have to look far for examples that sound much like the Pharisee's prayer. We can hear the echo of the Pharisee's prayer in many places. In Congress we might hear someone pray, "I thank you, Lord, that I am not like Democrats who compromise traditional values in a vain attempt to be relevant and popular." At the university we might hear someone pray, "I thank you, Lord, that I am not like conservatives who hold to mindless ideas that intelligent people don't believe any more." And in a local church we might hear someone pray, "I thank you, Lord, that I am not like liberal Christians who don't believe much of anything these days."

Then a long litany of credentials follows. The politician says, "I oppose abortion and want to abolish the Department of Education and support tax vouchers for private education." The university professor says, "I strive to have an open mind and celebrate diversity wherever I see it." And the evangelical Christian says, "I defend traditional morality and Christian beliefs, such as the virgin birth, the bodily resurrection of Christ, and the inerrancy of the Bible."

Not that standards of conduct and truth are relative. Once again, taken as a whole, the Pharisee lived in a way that was more healthy and helpful than the tax collector. As Lewis argued, the Pharisee was wrong not because of how he lived but because of his pride.

Helmut Thielicke, a German theologian who wrote brilliantly about the parables of Jesus, commented on the Pharisee's central problem:

> In the figure of the Pharisee we are confronted with a shocking exposure of the sin of Christianity, your sin and my sin, the sin of us who have subtly made of our Christianity a sign of virtue and given it the unpleasant smack of privilege. Pharisaic pride is one of the most dreadful and also one of the most infectious diseases of Christianity.[5]

OR ARE WE TAX COLLECTORS?

The tax collector, however, knew that he had reason to worry because he was a sinner. His standard of comparison was God. He was oblivious to the presence of the Pharisee in the temple. He was only aware of God. Again, Thielicke comments: "When a man really turns to God with a burdened conscience he doesn't think of other people at all. There he is utterly alone with God."[6] The tax collector never stated his specific need. We have no idea what his problem was—a nagging sin, a sick child, alienation from fellow Jews, disillusionment with his wealth.

Whatever his need, the tax collector stood in the presence of God, before whom he felt utterly inferior and unworthy. He hardly dared approach God. He didn't march to the front of the temple, as the Pharisee did, but remained in the back, where undesirables congregated. He was so overwhelmed by his shame that he stared at the ground, as if his eyes had been pulled down by the weight of his sin. He was so overcome by the gravity of his need that he beat his breast in contrition. Barely able to speak, he choked out a short, simple prayer. "God, have mercy on me, a sinner." His emptiness ran so deep that he could hardly name it, except to say that he needed God's mercy.

Jesus said that it was the tax collector's prayer that proved to be the acceptable one. He returned home right with God, not the Pharisee, because he knew his true need and admitted it.

The Heart of True Prayer

The heart of true prayer is this cry of desperation. There is a time and place in the Christian faith to master the techniques of prayer, to develop the discipline of prayer, and to become comfortable and confident when we pray. But what is most fundamental is the *spirit* of our prayers, the cry of the heart to get help from the only one who can meet our deepest need. Desperation is the first and primary condition for true prayer. The tax collector prayed out of desperation. He was in every other way unworthy of God, unqualified for prayer, and unacceptable to the religious community of Israel—and he knew it.

The reason why we don't pray more—and probably don't see more answers to prayer—is not because we don't know how to pray but because we don't really need to pray. We are not desperate enough.

The reason why we don't pray more—and probably don't see more answers to prayer—is not because we don't know how to pray but because we don't really need to pray. We are not desperate enough. It doesn't take much, however, to make us desperate. Each of us has a raw nerve that, once touched, drives us right to our knees.

I recently spoke at a retreat in the hill country of Texas. Dear friends drove me from the airport to the retreat center. They seemed to have everything—a gorgeous home on a 220-acre ranch overlooking a river, which became theirs through inheritance, professional success, a private plane, many friends, a wonderful family, and a great marriage. But last spring their college-age daughter was killed in a pedestrian accident. Three months later he was diagnosed with cancer.

Prosperity no longer matters much to them. They pray out of desperation.

A pastor I know married a woman with a troubled teenage son. A few months ago his stepson was shooting his shotgun at bottles outside the back door of their home. One of the bottles was full of rum. His mother went out to get the bottle. He demanded that she give it back, but she refused. So he took his shotgun and pointed it under his chin, threatening suicide. Then he pointed it at his mother, saying that he would kill her first. She pleaded with him to stop. He finally fired the gun just off her left shoulder, dropped it on the ground, and calmly walked away as if nothing had happened.

They immediately hid the gun and called the psychiatric ward at the local hospital. Then their son's biological father arrived. A long period of argument and negotiation followed. Finally, the son consented to be admitted into that ward. They found out later from a friend that he had tried to commit suicide several times before. They feel gratitude that he didn't kill anyone that day; they live in terror that he still could.

They pray out of desperation.

Caring parents who must send their children to schools overrun with gangs pray out of desperation. Families who have a child whose life is threatened with cancer pray out of desperation. Homeless teenagers who know that winter is coming pray out of desperation, and so do their mothers who long for them to return home. Diplomats who conduct negotiations to avert a war in some hotspot around the world pray out of desperation, as do the people who would be affected if a war does break out.

One of my favorite movies is *It's a Wonderful Life*. It tells the story of George Bailey, a good man who, for reasons beyond his control, is forced to remain in his hometown, Bedford Falls, to run the family business. He feels disappointed that his life did not turn out as he had dreamed. He never had a chance to travel the world and make a fortune. Instead, he chose loyalty and duty over adventure. He eventually marries, begins to raise a family, and serves the people around him.

One Christmas Eve day disaster strikes when his absent-minded uncle misplaces $8,000. Bailey searches for the money everywhere. He realizes that if he can't find the money, the family business will go under. He appeals for help to a competitor, an old, nasty, ruthless man, but he gleefully refuses, seeing his chance to drive Bailey out of business. When his competitor learns that Bailey has a modest life insurance policy, he says flippantly, "You are worth more dead than alive."

Bailey wanders off to a bar. He doesn't know what to do. He caresses the insurance policy stuffed into his coat pocket, pondering suicide. Then, slurping another drink, he tries to pray. "God, O God," he mutters under his breath, almost apologetically. "Dear Father in heaven. I'm not a praying man, but if you're up there and you can hear me, show me the way. I'm at the end of my rope. Show me the way, God."

Again, it is the cry of the heart, a prayer spoken out of desperation.

The Bible reminds us that desperate people pray because they have no other choice. They pray because they are starving; they pray because they face persecution; they pray because an army is about to overrun their village; they pray because they want their family to stay together. It is pray or go under, pray or despair, pray or die.

The New Testament is full of those kinds of prayers. Jairus, a man of reputation and influence, prayed because his daughter was sick and could not be cured, and no amount of wealth or power could save her.[7] A woman with an uncontrollable menstrual cycle prayed because every medical solution then in existence had failed her.[8] The thief on the cross prayed because he knew he was about to die, and no judicial pardon or stay of execution or miracle would allow him to put off having to face where he would spend eternity.[9]

None of these people knew how to pray with sophistication; none of them felt worthy or capable. They prayed out of desperation.

LEARNED DESPERATION

I prayed for my family before the accident, though I'm not sure I prayed out of desperation. But I do now, all the time. I might pray complacently about many things, but not about my children. I am so aware of my inadequacy as a father and of the long-term consequences of the trauma my children experienced that I find myself crying out to God as if God were my only hope, my last resort, my one chance to see that good triumphs over evil. I know how impermanent things are, how fragile relationships are, how little control I have.

Every time I watch my kids drive off in one of our cars, I tremble because I realize that I might never see them again, at least not in this life. As they grow up and prepare to leave the home, I worry because I know that they will face adversity, hardship, and temptation from which I cannot protect them. So I pray for them out of desperation. As a single father I know how much I need God.

But this is not the case all the time and in every situation. Not for me, and not for any of us. We may know we need God, but we don't always feel it. What do we do then?

When I was twenty-eight years old, I came down with a rare disease known as Rocky Mountain Spotted Fever. Doctors had trouble diagnosing what was wrong. By the time they did, I was deathly sick. I spent eight days in the intensive care unit. The medical staff had difficulty keeping my temperature below 105 degrees. My liver and kidneys failed, my heart stopped twice, and I had severe double pneumonia. I was close to death.

I still remember the desperation I felt to get enough air. I would take little gulps, but my lungs kept begging for more. I eventually recovered from the illness and started to breathe normally again. Ironically, I don't need air any less now than I did then. I was simply more aware of it. I was desperate for air, like a drowning man.

The same holds true with my need for God. Whether or not I feel it, my need for God is as great as my need for air, water, and food. Without God, I am dead.

The voice of the Pharisee in me will deny it. It evaluates my life according to human standards—how intelligent or clever or rich or moral or religious I am, at least in comparison to others. I usually come out on top when I think along those lines. The Pharisee in me tries to suppress the voice of the tax collector. But the tax collector's voice in me is the real and right one, and it tells me that my need for God is infinite and absolute. It tells me to pray, not merely as a pious exercise but as an expression of pure desperation. "If you don't pray," it says, "you will not make it."

So I pray, even when I don't feel like it. I pray for the growth of my students. I pray for the blessing and protection of God's people around the world. I pray for the healing of the sick, for reconciliation in relationships, for conversion of people who don't know Christ, both near and far, and for justice in the world. I pray for God's presence in the midst of struggle, tumult, and uncertainty. I pray for wisdom when I am confused. These are not casual prayers, though I often pray them casually, as if chatting politely with a stranger on an airplane to pass the time. If I would bother to think about it more often, I realize that these are weighty requests touching on significant issues. In the things that matter most, I am as needy as a newborn. We all are.

RISK OR SECURITY?

The security and prosperity we enjoy in life keeps us from seeing our real and raw need. Still, I'm not sure in the end that it really matters all that much. If anything, it's almost beside the point—for two reasons. First, there is far more to life than living comfortably and securely. Sometimes we settle for less than what God wants for us, and we fail to see what life could be if we really pursued God. We have blinders on. As Blaise Pascal once wrote, "We are far too easily pleased." We think that good health and material prosperity and nice friends are enough.

But God has something different—and better—planned. Once we grasp what God has in mind for us, then we will pray. We will pray for an awakening in our spiritual life. We will pray that the skeletons in the valley of dry bones may come to life. We will pray that God may make us the kind of people he has always intended us to be.

But there is a second reason why our own prosperity is irrelevant. The world is desperate, even if we are not. In the summer of 2000 my children and I traveled to Nairobi, Kenya, where we lived for two months. I taught at a university, and they did volunteer work at an orphanage founded by Mother Teresa. The orphanage was located in a huge slum of 250,000 people, an oasis of love in a desert of misery. My kids cared for the abandoned and disabled children who lived there. One orphan they met, already in her twenties, had lived there for as long as anyone could remember. She could not walk or sit up, dress herself, or feed herself. She just lay on a mat all day long. The nuns of that orphanage treated her with dignity and showed her great love.

Suddenly the needs of the world became more than a statistic. They stared us in the face; they had names and stories; they were real people, just like us. The gulf between their world and ours narrowed, at least for the short time we were there. Still, a trip to Kenya is hardly necessary. The City Gate is a few miles away. Needy neighbors live across the street. Lonely kids attend our schools. Unhappy homes beg for our attention. The cry of desperation echoes everywhere. The need is there, and so is the opportunity—if we are willing to expose ourselves to it.

Gordon MacDonald, a well-known writer and pastor, spent several days laboring with thousands of others at Ground Zero in the days following September 11. MacDonald had a profound experience there, different from what he had expected. He served in practical ways—carrying water for the bucket brigade and finding supplies that the workers needed. He also prayed for people, hundreds of them, who lined up to receive spiritual encouragement, like starving people at a soup kitchen. He was surprised by how eager people were for prayer. They were searching for God.

Strangely, it was MacDonald—the one who was there to pray for others—who wondered if God was there. How could God be present in the midst of all those traumatized and terrified people combing through the rubble, looking for survivors? The signs of death were everywhere. The heat, the smell, the dust, and the destruction were almost unbearable. It was a God-forsaken place, about as far removed from anything divine as hell is from heaven.

Yet MacDonald experienced God's presence. "I decided that God is closer to this place than any other place I've ever visited. . . . No church service; no church sanctuary; no religiously inspiring service has spoken so deeply into my soul and witnessed to the presence of God as those hours last night at the crash site."

But it was not just the presence of God he experienced in that setting, as devastating as it was. He also experienced vitality, power, a renewal of faith. "In all my years of Christian ministry, I never felt more alive than I felt last night. . . . As much as I love preaching the Bible and all the other things that I have been privileged to do over the years, being on that street, giving cold water to workmen, praying and weeping with them, listening to their stories was the closest I have ever felt to God. Even though it sounds melodramatic, I kept finding myself saying, 'This is the place where Jesus most wants to be.'"

Ironically, it is desperation itself—the true heart of prayer—that makes unanswered prayer so terrifying, wrenching, and disillusioning. There are few experiences more painful than having desperate prayers go unanswered. Hanging at the end of a rope over an abyss is bad enough; having someone cut the rope is even worse. But when God cuts the rope, it is worst of all. One would think that God would be more compassionate than that.

Desperation sets us up for a hard fall. What other options are left when our neediness drives us to God, but God doesn't respond to our need? It is like a parent's betrayal of a child, only worse, because God is supposed to know and do better. It is hard to fathom, hard to accept. We pray as the tax collector prayed: "God, have mercy on me, a sinner." We feel lost and needy, like someone wandering alone in the desert. We speak to God out of the deepest places of our hearts:

- "God, I need wisdom about this problem at work."
- "I want to experience your presence now that Mom has finally died."
- "I ask that you heal my son."
- "Please protect Sara and Bill, who have just been kidnapped in Bolivia."
- "Deliver Dad from his alcohol problem."
- "Dear God, I want to know that you are there for me, that everything will work out."

When these prayers are not answered as we ask, as we want, and as we need, we wonder whether God even hears or cares. We feel betrayed and utterly forsaken.

Desperation might be the true heart of prayer. But it is also a scourge and a terror. It makes us feel spiritually naked, utterly exposed, as if we were beetles flipped over on our backs, awaiting the inevitable stomp of a child's foot. Desperation forces us to pray as we ought. Desperation also makes us vulnerable to the disappointment of unanswered prayer. What do we do then?

QUESTIONS FOR DISCUSSION

1. Do you identify more with the Pharisee or the tax collector? Why?

2. What does it means to pray out of desperation?

3. When have you prayed out of desperation? What happened?

CHAPTER 3

CAN GOD TAKE
OUR COMPLAINTS?

The best prayers often have more groans than words.
JOHN BUNYAN

BEN WANDERHOPE IS A SINGLE FATHER WHO IS TRYING HIS BEST TO raise his teenage daughter, Carol, a challenging task even under the best of circumstances. But Wanderhope does not find himself in the best of circumstances. Carol has leukemia.

Wanderhope struggles to keep Carol going, and he struggles to keep himself going, too. He questions how God could allow such a thing to happen to his daughter. With Carol's life hanging in the balance, Wanderhope leaves the hospital and wanders into a church. In pure desperation he coughs out a prayer, half in belief and half in disbelief.

"I do not ask that she be spared to me," he says to God, "but that her life be spared to her. Or give us a year. We will spend it as we have the last, missing nothing." He describes to God how he will try to live that year, clinging to life as if it were his last breath. He promises that he will be a good father and take care of his beloved daughter. "All this we ask, with the remission of our sins, in Christ's name. Amen."[1]

Wanderhope returns to the hospital to discover that Carol is in remission. He is overcome with joy and gratitude, convinced God has answered his prayer. But within a day Carol contracts an infection ravaging the hospital and dies. He feels that God has teased and taunted him, feigning an answer to prayer, only in the end to kill her. He stares at Carol's lifeless body, stunned by the sudden and senseless death. "She looked finally like some mangled flower, or like a bird that had been pelted to earth in a storm. I knew that under the sheet she would look as though she had been clubbed to death."[2]

It is all too much for him. He makes his way back to the church. He finds the cake he accidentally left there, which he was going to give to Carol and the hospital staff to celebrate her remission. Leaving the church, he notices a crucifix hanging over the central doorway of the church. In his grief and rage he takes the cake, balances it perfectly in his hand, and flings it at the crucifix. His aim is perfect. The cake hits Jesus square in the face. Then Wanderhope sinks down to the steps, unable to move. He is utterly spent, having fought so hard, prayed so helplessly, hoped so foolishly for an answer to prayer that never came.

I have never hurled a cake at Jesus, as the fictional character Wanderhope does in Peter De Vries's wrenching novel *The Blood of the Lamb*. But I have wanted to because I have felt that same kind of emotion, that same kind of pain, that same kind of rage. Like Wanderhope, I have felt betrayed by God. Is it wrong to feel that kind of emotion? Is it wrong to vent that emotion to God?

EMOTION — RAW AND HUMAN

As human beings, we feel emotion as naturally as our noses smell or our ears hear. Emotion expresses what the heart feels. It is a reflex, the nervous system of the soul. It's a natural reaction to how we experience the world around us. When someone is kind to us, we feel grateful; when something good happens, we experience joy.

Likewise, when someone betrays us, we feel angry; when a friend dies, we feel sorrow; when tragedy strikes, we tremble with terror. We can't help but feel these emotions. Once we stop feeling, we stop living.

It is also natural to try to keep a lid on our emotions, especially if the emotion is negative. After all, who wants to spend their lives venting all the time? It's exhausting and offensive. But try as we might, emotion eludes easy control. It remains hidden in the shadows, waiting to pounce, sometimes when we least expect. One little thing can set us off, like a minor spat in a tense marriage that quickly erupts into a major blow-up.

My youngest child, John, was hurt seriously in the car accident. He was in traction for three weeks and in a full body cast for another nine weeks. He was two at the time, not yet potty trained. So we had to stuff diapers into a small opening in the cast. It didn't work very well. Then he got the flu. His temperature skyrocketed. He suffered from severe cramps, nausea, diarrhea, and dehydration. His sickness was all too much for me, like the proverbial straw that broke the camel's back.

I was so distressed, so angry, so bewildered that I cried uncontrollably, raging against my circumstances. The accident had been enough, I thought. John's injury had made matters worse. Now this! I thought my life was on a downward spiral that would never end until it crashed on the ground. How could this be happening? How could God allow this to happen? What kind of sadistic God would watch and witness our family's suffering and do nothing about it?

HURTING THE INNOCENT

The real question, then, is not whether we have emotion but what we should do with it. There are several bad alternatives.

First, we can try to suppress emotion, which only puts a cork on a bottle bound to explode, sooner or later. A husband suppresses his growing irritation at his wife's spending habits. Then, when she brings home a new pair of gloves, he expresses a rage that far exceeds what seems appropriate, considering the cost of the gloves. Or a mother suppresses her disappointment at her daughter's indifferent academic performance. Then, when she gets a C on one biology quiz, she goes on a tirade and grounds her daughter for a month from all activities.

Suppression might work, but only for a while. In the end emotion will always break loose and strike, sometimes when we least expect it, like a domesticated animal that fights back when cornered because it has never lost its wildness.

Second, we can lash out at innocent bystanders, expressing our emotion in the wrong way, at the wrong time, and to the wrong person, like the teenager who picks on his little sister because he detests himself for his own obesity or the coach who punishes the team because he is sick of losing. This kind of misdirected hostility only exacerbates the pain. It is like civilian deaths in a war. It is bad enough when the enemy has to die. How much worse it is when innocents die, either accidentally or intentionally. Does it have to be that way?

Third, we can turn our emotion inward and punish ourselves, assuming—rightly—that we ought to take responsibility for mistakes we have made. Shame is a real and healthy emotion that can lead to confession and responsibility. But feelings of shame can far exceed what is healthy and normal, leading (among other things) to depression. Depression is often the consequence of anger turned inward, smothering all joy, peace, and forgiveness.

Years ago a family friend of ours, driving home from work, struck a boy riding his bicycle. The boy darted between two parked cars and drove right into the path of our friend's oncoming car. There was nothing our friend could have done to avoid hitting the boy. It was an accident, tragic but unavoidable. But that provided no comfort for him. He felt deep regret, guilt, and depression, which did not subside over time. He punished himself until the day he died.

AN ASSAULT ON GOD

There is a better way. We can vent our emotion toward heaven so that everything we spew—bitterness and hatred and revenge and despair—never touches anyone else. This assault on heaven seems audacious and irreverent, as inappropriate as desecrating the cross. Yet the Bible invites us to do just that. The Psalms, all 150 of them, provide a model for us. They show us how to express our emotions, not only positive ones, like gladness and gratitude, but negative ones, like anger and despair.

The Psalms remind us that we don't need to be in a "good place" to pray. Where we are is the right place, no matter how bad the place might be. Any prayer, as it turns out, is better than no prayer at all. Though it is right to show reverence toward God, it is also permissible to express anger and despair. At the least, it demonstrates that we are taking God seriously enough to communicate with him.

John Calvin, a leader of the sixteenth-century Protestant Reformation and a stoic if there ever was one, appreciated the Psalms for this very reason. "I have been accustomed," he wrote in his preface to his commentary on the Psalms,

> to call this book, I think not inappropriately, "An Anatomy of all the Parts of the Soul;" for there is not an emotion of which any one can be conscious that is not here represented as in a mirror. Or rather, the Holy Spirit has here drawn to the life all the griefs, sorrows, fears, doubts, hopes, cares, perplexities, in short, all the distracting emotions with which the minds of men are wont to be agitated.[3]

The Psalms put negative emotions into words. Half the Psalms contain complaints, usually directed toward God. The psalmist does not hesitate to wrestle with God, cry out to God, weep before God, even blame God for misery and suffering. However high their view of God, the Hebrews believed that God was great and gracious enough to absorb this raw and reckless emotion and strong enough to withstand the hostility we pour on him. The Psalms show us that, when we approach God, we must speak the truth—about ourselves, about our circumstances, especially about our feelings. God doesn't seem to take offense. If anything, he invites such expression. He wants us to turn our emotion into a prayer, however nasty it might be. Listen to these cries:

O LORD, how many are my foes!
  How many rise up against me
Many are saying of me,
  "God will not deliver him.[4]

"I am worn out from groaning;
  all night long I flood my bed with weeping
  and drench my couch with tears.
My eyes grow weak with sorrow.[5]

Why, O LORD, do you stand far off?
  Why do you hide yourself in times of trouble?[6]

O LORD God Almighty,
  how long will your anger smolder
  against the prayers of your people?
You have fed them with the bread of tears;
  you have made them drink tears by the bowlful.[7]

Does our emotion hurt God? Of course it does. Still, God is able to absorb our emotion and love us, even when we rage against him. God is like a good parent who is not put off when a frustrated child screams, "I hate you, I hate you, I hate you," to his mom because she put him to bed early for not completing his chores. God allows us to pour out our hearts to him and get rid of the poison, regardless of how much there is, so that it can be diluted in the ocean of his love.

I found that venting my emotion to God brought great release and relief to me after the accident. Little problems, like John's sickness, occurred often and disrupted the fragile equilibrium of our home. I would try my best to maintain stability until the kids were in bed. Then I would fall on my face and cry out to God, blaming him for my pain and misery. I pushed him with hard questions: "Why are you allowing this to happen?" Rightly or wrongly, I challenged the integrity of his character, calling him a bully and brute. As I look back now, I realize that I was probably wrong to charge God so ruthlessly. Yet I was so distraught, angry, and confused that I had to do *something* with my emotions. I decided to pour it out to God. "I would never treat anyone like you are treating me," I coughed out through the tears. "Pick on somebody your own size. Leave me alone. I want nothing to do with you."

The Psalms provided me with the language of complaint that I needed, thus inviting me to spit my accusations at God. The language is not bleached of power, as much of the clinical language we use today is. I found biblical language truer to my own experience. We use a clinical word like "depression," but the Psalms use words like "pit" and "darkness." We speak of "loss," but the Psalms talk about walking through "the valley of the shadow of death." No clinical language is as visceral and powerful as these lines from Psalm 22: "I am poured out like water, and all my bones are out of joint. My heart has turned to wax; it is melted away within me . . . my tongue sticks to the roof of my mouth."[8] If we want to use language that expresses human emotion, we must resort to poetry, metaphor, and analogy, not clinical description. The Psalms equip us with such language.

EMOTION AS A PRAYER

The Psalms invite us to channel our emotions toward God and to turn them into a prayer, so that in the end our emotions enrich our relationship with God. That we pray *honestly* seems to be as important as praying properly. Whether expressing praise or rage, prayer does accomplish at least one thing—it pushes us toward God. As I tell young couples preparing for marriage, one thing is worse than fighting, and that is not communicating at all. Better to fight it out until you reach resolution than to give up altogether. The Psalms encourage us to fight it out—with God.

God welcomes honesty because he is a God of truth. Calling us to live by truth, God wants us to live in truth, to speak truth, to pursue truth, regardless of the consequences. Moreover, God despises hypocrisy. Hypocrites give the appearance of something that is simply not true deep inside the heart. They are nice to bosses face-to-face but mock them behind their back, give the appearance of being happy in public when they are constantly crabby at home, and say one thing while doing another. Hypocrites play religion on Sunday mornings but ignore God the rest of the week.

The Psalms invite us to channel our emotions toward God and to turn them into a prayer, so that in the end our emotions enrich our relationship with God.

God can't do much with hypocrites until they are willing to admit the truth about themselves. However uncomfortable expressing the truth, they must do so anyway. They must be honest about their circumstances, honest about themselves, and honest about God, even if their honesty has an edge to it. How can the self ever change if it is not willing to tell the truth first?

John Chrysostom advised that true prayer should express what is in the depths of the human heart. If anyone understood suffering, surely it was John Chrysostom. When serving as a pastor in Antioch in the late fourth century, he was called to preach every day to a traumatized congregation, some of whom were being executed by the Roman emperor in retaliation for a riot that broke out in the city. Then, years later, while serving as Patriarch of Constantinople, the empress banished him from civilization for criticizing her immoral lifestyle. That banishment led to his death.

Yet he never stopped praying. When he prayed during the many crises he faced, he told God the truth. "I am talking of prayer which rises from the bottom of the heart. . . . If you share with your master the suffering you feel in your soul, it is much surer that you will receive confirmation and consolation in abundance."[9]

EVEN JESUS COMPLAINED!

Surely Jesus himself is our model. He, too, was honest with God and expressed his emotions. After eating with his disciples, Jesus took them to Gethsemane, where he prayed in agony to his Father in heaven, asking that the cup of suffering pass from him. Matthew says that Jesus was "sorrowful and troubled." He "fell with his face to the ground" to pray. Luke adds that "his sweat was like drops of blood falling to the ground."[10]

Just a few hours later Jesus was crucified. He hung on that cross like a spectacle in a freak show, mocked by the masses and utterly forsaken by his friends. The Gospels record only seven sentences that Jesus spoke during those six or so agonizing hours. One was a direct quote from Psalm 22. Jesus used a psalm to express his fear, his confusion, and his pain. He called his Father in heaven to account. "My God, my God, why have you forsaken me?"[11] One of many psalms of complaint, Psalm 22 rings with wrenching despair because the Psalmist feels as if God has abandoned him. If Jesus had had enough breath and strength, he might have recited the entire Psalm, for the Psalm describes the kind of ordeal that Jesus faced.

> *My God, my God, why have you forsaken me?*
>   *Why are you so far from helping me, from the words*
>   *of my groaning?*
> *O my God, I cry by day, but you do not answer;*
>   *and by night, but find no rest.*
>
> *But I am a worm, and not human;*
>   *scorned by others, and despised by the people.*
> *All who see me mock at me;*
>   *they make mouths at me, they shake their heads.*

For dogs are all around me;
a company of evildoers encircles me.
My hands and feet have shriveled;
I can count all my bones.[12]

Astonishing as it may seem, Jesus himself did not hesitate to express his anguish and forsakenness before his Father in heaven. But in using this psalm, he turned his emotion into a prayer. His emotion drove him to God.

It doesn't matter what the emotion is, either. The Psalms give voice to a wide range of emotions. It could be confusion because God seems distant and silent. The Psalmist cries out to God for deliverance, but God does nothing, like a passive observer who witnesses a mugging and turns his back on it.

But I cry to you for help, O LORD;
in the morning my prayer comes before you.
Why, O LORD, do you reject me
and hide your face from me?[13]

It could be bitterness because God has allowed enemies to prosper at the Psalmist's expense (Psalm 73; 109) and has allowed even his friends to betray him (Psalm 55). It could be revenge because the Psalmist wants to strike back at those who have hurt him (Psalm 137). It could be despair because the Psalmist doesn't know what to do in the face of God's apparent indifference (Psalm 77:1–10).

CALLING GOD TO ACCOUNT!

All these emotions are brought to God and leveled against him, as if God himself were at fault. Many Psalms demonstrate utter audacity because they fire their complaints at God. They seem as unreligious as atheism, as ruthless as the devil. The Psalms charge God with wrongdoing; they hold God responsible for suffering and anguish. If anyone is to blame, it is God. He seems to be responsible for a great deal of the suffering, death, and destruction that occurs in the world. Reflecting on the ravages of the Black Death in the late 1350s, which wiped out a third of the population of Europe, Connie Willis writes in her novel *Doomsday Book,* "It was God who should have to beg forgiveness."[14]

Surprisingly, God seems to look with compassion and favor on those who accuse him and yell at him. For example, Job did not hesitate to shake his fist at God for the losses he suffered, all in his mind undeserved, though God did call Job to account for his accusations. Jacob spent a whole night wrestling with God, refusing to give up even after God disabled him. Jeremiah seemed to complain about everything, and with good reason, considering the suffering he had to endure. Naomi changed her name to Mara, which means "bitterness," because she believed that God had abandoned her to a lifetime of misery and misfortune. What God can't tolerate is a plastic saint, a polite believer, someone who plays a part but never gets inside the soul of the character. God prefers working with people who like to fight.

Leif Enger's *Peace Like a River* tells the story of an unusual family of four: Jeremiah, the father, and his three children, Davy, Swede, and Reuben, who narrates the story. Davy gets himself into serious trouble. He is arrested and put on trial. Knowing that the jury is about to convict him, he breaks out of a county jail and flees. A few weeks later the rest of the family piles into an Airstream trailer and goes in search of him.

Jeremiah is a praying man. He is humble, discerning, and submissive. But he reaches a point where he can't understand what God is up to. He senses that God wants him to cooperate with a federal agent who is hunting for Davy. This seems preposterous to him. He resents the idea, considering it an affront and a betrayal. So he decides to have it out with the Almighty. He stays up all night and fights it out with God in prayer.

Reuben recounts what was later told to him by a friend, Roxanna, who sat in the hallway and overheard the argument. She, of course, only heard one side, Jeremiah's. She was not privy to God's voice, though she knew that God was speaking and fighting back.

> At this Roxanna covered her mouth, for it occurred to her with Whom he wrestled. Having long ago accepted the fact of God, Roxanna had not conceived of going toe to toe with Him over a particular concern. *Make me willing if you can,* Dad cried, a challenge it still shakes me to think of. What Roxanna heard next was a tumble like a man thrown.

And so the conflict between God and Jeremiah continued through the night. Roxanna eventually fell asleep in the hallway. When she awoke in the morning all was quiet. She went into the kitchen and found Jeremiah sitting at the kitchen table. He was at peace, having wrestled with God until an answer came and direction was clear. This praying man did not hesitate to take God on, though of course he learned that one cannot win an argument with the Almighty.[15]

Sometimes there seems to be good reason to pick a fight with God. God doesn't always appear to behave much like God is supposed to. Christians believe that God is transcendent, holy, and powerful. God holds the universe in his hand, guides history according to his perfect will, and rules over the affairs of humanity. He is in control! It seems to follow, therefore, that if someone suffers, it is ultimately God's doing. God could do something to help if he wanted to. If nothing happens, it is because God chooses to do nothing.

So the Psalmist rightly accuses God, rages against God, and calls God into question.

> *Why, O LORD, do you stand far off?*
> *Why do you hide yourself in times of trouble?[16]*

> *How long, O LORD? Will you forget me forever?*
> *How long will you hide your face from me?*
> *How long must I wrestle with my thoughts,*
> *and every day have sorrow in my heart?*
> *How long will my enemy triumph over me?[17]*

O Lord, do not rebuke me in your anger
or discipline me in your wrath.
For your arrows have pierced me,
and your hand has come down upon me.[18]

Elie Wiesel, Holocaust survivor and author of many books on suffering, including the classic *Night,* recounts a trial held in a German death camp during the war. What made the trial so strange was the identity of the accused. The rabbis put God on trial. For three days they presented the evidence to a jury. Witnesses told stories of their suffering. They recounted how they had prayed to God, but God had done nothing to answer their prayers, to deliver them from their misery, and to defend their just cause. The jury found God guilty. When the trial was over, the rabbis prayed to the very God whom they had just convicted. As a witness to the trial, Wiesel decided then and there to tell the story if he ever survived his ordeal.

But he decided that he would want to include another character, a defense lawyer. The defense lawyer would present evidence and arguments for God's innocence. He would say that, though God cared about the Jews, he lacked the power to do something about it or that, though God had the power to do something, he chose to let events take their own course.

That defense lawyer, Wiesel believed, would be the devil himself because only the devil would think to defend God by diminishing his sovereignty or his goodness. Rather than blame God, as the Psalmist does, the devil would want to excuse God as weak or incompetent, someone hardly worth taking seriously.

> *The God depicted in the Psalms is big enough to absorb our accusations and to take full responsibility for the suffering of the world.*

The Psalms will have nothing to do with that kind of God. The God depicted in the Psalms is big enough to absorb our accusations and to take full responsibility for the suffering of the world. The Psalms put God squarely at the center of the problem. Unanswered prayer is God's problem. God is good, sovereign, and wise, responsible for running the universe. His sovereign and gracious will is supposed to prevail, especially when we cry to him. If something goes wrong, God is to blame, or so the Psalmist believes.

RESOLUTION AND TRIUMPH

But the Psalms do not end on such a pessimistic note. The act of wrestling with God leads to resolution, struggle gives way to peace, accusations turn into submission. The yelling finally stops, and quiet returns to the Psalmist's soul. The one who writes, "Why, O LORD, do you stand far off?" concludes his psalm:

> O LORD, you will hear the desire of the meek;
>   you will strengthen their heart, you will incline your ear
> to do justice for the orphan and the oppressed,
>   so that those from earth may strike terror no more.[19]

Such resolution is never more startling and moving than the testimony of the writer of Psalm 22, the very psalm Jesus had on his lips as he was dying on the cross. This psalm expresses both despair and hope, anger and faith. The cry of pain ends with a confession of confidence; agony leads to resolution. If there is no struggle, there can be no peace. The Psalmist won't have one without the other.

He begins with an accusation. "My God, my God, why have you forsaken me?" He rails against God for the pain and anguish he feels, like a child who finally gets a chance to strike out against an abusive parent. He feels utterly abandoned. The pain is too much for him to bear.

Yet in the end he confesses his faith in the same God he accuses, he prays for deliverance to the same God who has made his life so miserable. However angry, he recognizes that apart from God there is no help and no hope.

But you, O LORD, do not be far off;
  O my Strength, come quickly to help me.
Deliver my life from the sword,
  my precious life from the power of the dogs.
Rescue me from the mouth of the lion.[20]

The Psalmist believes, though he has no apparent reason to, that God will hear his prayer and rescue him, that God will come through because God is faithful and good. He seems almost wild with joy. He is confident that, in spite of his dire circumstances, God is still in control:

I will declare your name to my brothers [and sisters];
  in the congregation I will praise you.
You who fear the LORD, praise him!
  All you descendants of Jacob, honor him!
  Revere him, all you descendants of Israel!

All the ends of the earth
  will remember and turn to the LORD,
and all the families of the nations
  will bow down before him,
for dominion belongs to the LORD
  and he rules over the nations.[21]

The Psalms keep us grounded in God. Every home needs a grounding wire to keep it safe during an electrical storm. However powerful the strike of lightning, it will inflict no damage if a home has such a wire, for that wire will send the electrical charge directly into the ground, where it can do no damage. The Psalms are like grounding wire for emotional lightning bolts.

The Psalms invite us to complain, to plot revenge, to accuse God, all in the form—amazing as this sounds—of a prayer. The Psalms assume that God is big enough, powerful enough, and gracious enough to absorb that emotion so that it causes no destruction. Ironically, the frustration that unanswered prayer engenders is

The Psalms invite us to complain, to plot revenge, to accuse God, all in the form—amazing as this sounds—of a prayer.

itself turned into a prayer. Rather than cutting us off from God, unanswered prayer drives us to God. These prayers might sound as bitter as poison, but they are still prayers. It seems as if any kind of prayer, even those that are mean and angry, is better than no prayer at all. However irreverent, these prayers are still prayers.

God can take our complaints. He even welcomes our complaints. He tells us to express our frustration directly to him, even when it involves what appears to be his own failure.

Still, that doesn't really solve the problem of unanswered prayer. It mollifies the emotions that bubble up when our prayers go unanswered. It allows us to take that emotion directly to God. All that is good and helpful, like learning to fight fair with a spouse after years of hiding our emotion. But once rid of the emotions, we are still stuck with the problem. What do we do about unanswered prayer?

QUESTIONS FOR DISCUSSION

1. Can you recount experiences you have had that awakened deep emotion? What kinds of emotions, both negative and positive, did you feel?

2. Read Psalm 22. How does the Psalmist describe his experience? What emotions does he express? What kind of resolution does he come to?

3. How can venting emotion to God actually enrich one's relationship with God?

4. What kinds of emotions do you feel the need to express to God at this point of your life?

CHAPTER 4

THE GIFT OF
UNANSWERED PRAYER

*I have lived to thank God that all my prayers
have not been answered.*
JEAN INGELOW

IT IS EVERY MOTHER'S WORST NIGHTMARE.

She is the mother of a little boy, Kostya, who is only three years old. Kostya is dying of an incurable disease. The mother believes in God, and she believes that God can heal her little boy. She alternates agonizingly between hope and despair, fighting and giving up. Still, she prays, "imbuing her prayer with all the power of her soul, although somewhere deep within her she feared that God would not move the mountain—that he would act not according to her desires, but according to his own will."[1]

Her little boy dies. *Why?* she thinks to herself.

Why would the God to whom I prayed so much allow him to die? Why? Did my boy bother anyone? Did he do anything bad to anybody? Doesn't God know that he was my whole life, that I can't live without him? And then to suddenly take and torture this helpless, innocent little creature and shatter my life and answer all my prayers with his lifeless eyes, with his cold, stiff body. . . . Why pray to God if he can do such terrible things?[2]

Leo Tolstoy tells this woman's story in a short story entitled "Prayer," which he wrote after reading about a shipwreck in the United States in which many children died. Tolstoy wrote the story to explore the problem of unanswered prayer. I read the story only recently, when I was pondering the problem myself. I once thought that unanswered prayer was either the result of God's sovereign will, which functions like a trump card, making our prayers largely irrelevant, or the result of human failure, which makes our prayers unacceptable to God, however needy we are. In either case, the outcome is the same—unanswered prayer.

A Startling Idea

Tolstoy put me onto a new idea, both troubling and helpful. *What would happen*, I wondered, *if all our prayers were answered?*

I searched my memory, trying to recall some of the prayers I prayed many years ago. I thought about the early and heady years of serving as a youth pastor in southern California when I was ready to conquer the world, with or without Christ. Though the church at which I served was healthy and growing, the youth program I inherited was a wreck. I realized at once that I faced an enormous challenge, just the kind of problem that made my blood run. I recruited several volunteers my own age who were as outrageous and audacious as I was. We abolished the old program, waited three months, and then started a new program called FUDD (Fishermen's Union of Dedicated Disciples). The new program struck us as cool as surfing at Huntington Beach.

We faced immediate resistance. Some parents were concerned about the demands we were putting on the kids, and some kids didn't like the emphasis on outreach. Parents complained; kids dropped out. We prayed with boldness and passion that God would bless our work. After nine months of hard and fruitless labor, we held a weekend retreat in the mountains. Forty-five students attended, a huge number to us. The weekend was electric, the quintessential mountaintop experience. Perhaps twenty students became Christians that weekend; many others experienced renewal. The momentum of that retreat continued for a long time. Within two years the high school group grew from twenty members to 125. It was *the* group in the area to attend. I was riding a wave of success. I witnessed many answers to prayer and enjoyed the fruits of my labor. Everything I touched turned into gold.

Eventually the ministry leveled off and lost momentum. And thank God it did, for I had become insufferably proud, a self-appointed expert in youth ministry. I wonder what would have happened to me had all my prayers been answered during those early years of ministry, if our group had continued to grow, if our program had continued to receive recognition. Perhaps unanswered prayer was good for me.

In his short story Tolstoy introduces a character, Mary, who is a nurse's aide and also an angel. Mary provides a divine perspective on the mother's loss. Could it be, Tolstoy asks, that unanswered prayer serves our own best interest? Instead of looking at unanswered prayer as the problem, Tolstoy explores whether *answered* prayer might be the problem. Could it be that unanswered prayer is a strange kind of gift?

That we pray does not in and of itself make us saints, for our prayers are often imbued with selfishness. When we pray, we pray not only as saints but also as sinners, very much inclined to use prayer to advance our own selfish interests, even when we pray out of desperation. Prayer for that reason is highly complex. On the one hand, the very act of praying reminds us that we are children of God. On the other hand, that same act of praying exposes us for the fallen creatures we are. As strange as it may sound, answered prayer could actually exacerbate the very problem in us—namely, sin—that God has acted in Jesus Christ to remedy, like a new medication that produces side-effects worse than the disease itself.

Thus, some prayers God won't or can't answer, for our own good. To answer these kinds of prayers would be bad for us and unworthy of God. We should never forget, especially when we pray, that we are sinful, fallible creatures, utterly dependent on God for life and salvation. When we pray, we should never forget the vast difference between God and us.

Our prideful prayers put God into a dilemma—if he fails to answer our prayers, God appears mean and distant; if he answers our prayers, we end up worse off than before.

There is something in us, however, that causes us to forget. It is our pride, which, as the worst of the deadly sins, insidiously hides behind behaviors that appear as good, even religious practice. Pride tempts all of us to use prayer for base purposes. When we pray, therefore, we angle for things that would not be good for us or pleasing to God, even when we pray out of genuine neediness. Ironically, pride will take answers to our most desperate prayers and exploit them for some unworthy purpose.

Our prideful prayers put God into a dilemma—if he fails to answer our prayers, God appears mean and distant; if he answers our prayers, we end up worse off than before.

WINNERS AND LOSERS

Prayer reinforces pride in at least two situations. The first occurs when we pray for victory at someone else's expense. Such prayers strive to make us winners and our opponents losers. We thus force God to take sides in a contest or dispute or conflict we want to win, at all costs. As Mary says to the distraught mother in Tolstoy's short story, "You should not be angry with God. He cannot listen to everyone. Sometimes people hear only one side, and in order to do good for one the other is abused."[3]

But what if people from the other side are praying for victory, too? If two people pray for opposite things, then God cannot answer both prayers at the same time. The requests are mutually exclusive. If God answered both, then he would contradict himself. So one person at least—and perhaps both—will be disappointed because God doesn't answer her or their prayers. It could be that God doesn't take sides at all, at least not in the way we would like.

Perhaps the people who attribute victory to God are giving God credit for something he didn't do. In situations involving a win or a loss, God might actually stand on the side of those who lose. He might be eager to answer their prayers because his ear is turned toward the cry of the weak and desperate. Besides, it could be that the loss propelled them to pray for what matters most in God's eyes—humility, courage, and patience. We must beware, in other words, of assuming that God is on our side when we win and not on the side of those who lose, as if victory implies God's favor and loss means God's rejection. Then again, we must be equally cautious about assuming that, because God takes the side of those who lose, he always opposes those who win. Perhaps God doesn't think in terms of losing or winning at all, at least not in the way we are inclined to.

When my oldest son, David, was in elementary school, he played on a soccer team that dominated the city league. At one point his team won twenty straight matches, culminating in a victory in the city tournament at season's end. But during the following year David's team lost four matches in a row, including one lopsided loss to a team that had never beaten them. That team gloated and taunted David and his teammates after the match, which only made matters worse.

David's team rallied during the final city tournament, however, playing well enough to make it into the finals. To their dismay, they had to square off against the team that had beaten them so badly only a few weeks before. Both teams played well. At the end of regulation play, the score was tied two to two. So the teams had to go into a shoot-out. A shoot-out requires five players from each team to shoot against the opposing goalkeeper from twelve yards out. Whichever team scores the most goals in the shootout wins the match.

By this time the parents on our side had turned the match into something akin to a medieval crusade, complete with all the spiritual overtones. I heard several parents mutter, "Please, Lord, let our boys win." One woman said, "God, if they win, I will believe in you again." Not to be outdone, I—a seasoned Christian, an ordained minister, an author of books on theology, a professor with a Ph.D.— joined this chorus of prayer and even conjured up several reasons why God should answer our prayers.

Our team won when our goalkeeper blocked the last shot. The kids went wild, leaping into the air and piling on top of each other. It looked like a scene from a Disney movie. One parent said, "I believe there's a God again." Being more modest and pious, I simply uttered a prayer of thanksgiving under my breath.

We had no way of knowing, of course, what was happening on the other side of the field. I learned more about the other team only recently, some five years later, when I met a Christian parent from the opposing side. In the course of our conversation she described a tournament in which her son had played years earlier. At first I had no idea that she was talking about the famous match.

Her son's team, she reported, had suffered a "devastating" loss in the finals. As she described it, their team had been a perennial loser, especially to one particular team that had "no idea what it felt like to lose." Their team had finally beaten this nemesis, and badly, too. They had to face the same team again in the tournament finals. Their team "needed" that victory, she said, to add the finishing touches to the only winning season they had ever had. But they lost—"in a shootout," she said, "and on the last shot." Only then did I realize that she was talking about the same match.

Did God answer our prayers and deny theirs? I don't think so. For all I know, God answered their prayers in a more significant way. Perhaps they had been praying that their sons would grow up well, learning to honor God, to become people of character, and to develop perspective in life so that winning or losing a soccer match would become less and less important. Adversity, after all, probably does more to help people grow up than easy victories. In the end losing might have been better for them than winning was for us.

As I look back now, I think that our prayers were silly, short-sighted, and selfish. But is that really surprising? We often say selfish prayers without thinking much about them. We pray for parking spaces when we're running late, never considering that ten other people, as late as we are, might be praying, too, for the two remaining spaces available in the parking garage. We pray for victories in elections, forgetting that victory for one party means defeat for another party that might be just as prayerful as we are. We pray for success in business, though increased sales in our business might undermine competitors down the street who are praying for the same thing and need success more than we do. Not that these prayers are necessarily wrong, but we should remember that answers to our prayers might be at someone else's expense.

These are innocent examples. But not every case is so innocent. Sometimes people pray for victory when the stakes are high and prayer seems like the only alternative to despair and defeat. Christians on opposing sides have prayed for victory in conflicts that were—and are—far more serious and deadly. Some Christians in the United States are praying for Israel's victory over the Palestinians, while Christians in Palestine are praying not for victory but for peace. Again, some Christians in Northern Ireland are praying for the defeat of "the enemy," whether Protestant or Catholic, while other Christians are praying not for vindication but for reconciliation. And some Christians in the United States are praying for economic recovery in our nation, while Christians in other parts of the world are praying for enough food to survive another day.

The same problem occurred during the Civil War. Both North and South claimed that God was on their side, quoted from the same

Bible but came to opposite conclusions, and prayed for victory over their fellow countrymen. Obviously, God could not answer every one of their prayers.

Ironically, Abraham Lincoln, the only president who never joined a church (though he did attend a Presbyterian church) and who was often accused of being irreligious, expressed probably the most profound theological analysis of the war. While Christians from both sides claimed that God was on their side, Lincoln wondered whether God was on either side. "Both [sides] read the same Bible, and pray to the same God; and each invokes His aid against the other. It may seem strange that any man should dare to ask a just God's assistance in wringing their bread from the sweat of other men's faces. . . . The prayers of both could not be answered; that of neither has been answered fully. The Almighty has His own purposes."

We pray for victory, as does the other side. But how do we know that we are right and the other side wrong? Even if we are right—clearly there are occasions when one side is right and the other side is wrong!—God may still have a purpose in mind that transcends our own. Besides, it is possible to be perfectly right on a superficial level and yet wrong in the things that matter most in life. At the least, then, we must be humble when we pray, recognizing that God is sovereign. Though victory for one side may be good and right, that victory may still play a small role in a much bigger plan God is working out. God may takes sides, but not necessarily our side, even if, as is sometimes the case, we are actually right.

That is the danger of praying for victory. Our cause may be right, in a narrow sense. But we may still be wrong in a larger sense—manifesting pride, gloating in victory, punishing wrongdoers with excessive severity, and excusing sin. The great hazard for people on a crusade is that, however legitimate the crusade, they become blind to their own faults. So confident are they of being right and of having God on their side that they lose the capacity to discover that they may be wrong, too. They oppose abortion but don't care about the needs of women. They fight for civil rights but treat secretaries and janitors like second-class citizens. They uphold the standards of biblical sexuality but show little grace toward their spouses and children.

So when we pray for victory, as sometimes we must, we should always, always pray with humility. Otherwise the "victories" we gain will be Pyrrhic only, won at too great a cost. What does it profit, asks Jesus, if we gain the whole world—winning every conflict in which we are engaged—but lose our own soul?

POWER AT TOO HIGH A COST

Thus praying for victory at someone else's expense is the first occasion when our prayers might not be answered. The second occasion occurs when answers to prayer would lead to our spiritual ruin. Again, I have only recently wrestled with this problem.

I have known for many years that power is dangerous, even for those who seem to have a good reason to assert it. Both experience and history teach us this. Economic power (e.g., wealth) can make people materialistic and greedy; political power (elected office) can serve petty and selfish interests; intellectual power (academic posts) can capitulate to ideology and thus fail to search for truth; military power can bully and punish for wrongs, whether done or not done. History contains too many examples of power gone bad, ruining the people who had it. All forms of power are inherently dangerous.

We usually think ourselves to be the exception to the rule. I know I do. I am confident, in my self-delusion, that power would not corrupt me because I think I am nearly always right, very wise, and so capable of wielding it. So, if I had power, I would use it responsibly, never mind the failures of everyone else. But it is easy to be altruistic in theory, when I am speculating about what I would do with power if I had it. It is hard to be altruistic in fact.

When we have no money, we say we would be generous if we had some; but then we find good reasons to spend money on ourselves when our income rises, which is why the least generous people (at least in terms of percentage of income given) are the rich. We claim that we will uphold the cause of justice before we enter politics; but then, once we assume office, we use the office to serve our own interests. We imagine ourselves courageously pursuing truth when we first enter the field of higher education; but by the time we have earned tenure, we are caught up in the latest intellectual fashion and conceit. We are almost completely incapable of using power for a greater good.

When Lynda and I were first married, we barely scraped by on my feeble income. We had to pinch pennies to contribute a tithe to the church. Now, years later, my income is far greater. I have enough money for both needs and wants, with some left over. Yet I find it harder now to give than I did years ago, when I lived in virtual poverty. More money has not made me more generous, at least not in my heart.

I am also a full professor, having progressed through the various ranks until I can rise no further. I used to ponder what it would be like to hold the highest rank at the college. I imagined giving generously of my time to the college, volunteering for administrative tasks, and mentoring new colleagues. Yet I am more jealous of my time now, more wary of taking on projects that do not serve my own scholarly interests, and more protective of programs and courses I have developed. I have to force myself to share the power I have, to make room for new blood and new ideas.

The Danger of Spiritual Power

Surprisingly, spiritual power can be as dangerous as any other kind of power. The primary means of access to spiritual power, of course, is prayer. When we pray, we call upon a transcendent God to use his power to perform some good deed—to heal a loved one who is sick, to give us wisdom when making a decision, to prosper a new ministry, to defend the cause of justice, to give us influence in the world.

For a long time I did not recognize the danger of spiritual power. It hadn't occurred to me that spiritual power, the power we access through prayer, is as corruptible as any other form of power, if not more so.

Perhaps no writer in the twentieth century has explored the corrosive nature of power, including spiritual power, more than J. R. R. Tolkien, author of the famous *The Lord of the Rings* trilogy. Tolkien did not write the trilogy in a vacuum. He had experienced the ravages of two world wars. The first war in particular, fought between supposedly Christian empires, exacted a huge toll in human life (ten million dead) and raised haunting questions in his mind about power.

Tolkien wrote the trilogy to explore this theme, among others. Sauron, an evil sorcerer, forges twenty magical rings—three for the elves, seven for the dwarves, and nine for human kings. But he keeps one for himself, and this ring, "the one to rule them all and in the darkness bind them," is the most powerful of all. It controls the others.

This ring serves as a metaphor for supernatural power that intoxicates, perverts, and destroys. No matter how well intentioned, the person who possesses this one ring will eventually use it for evil purposes. There appears to be no exceptions to that rule. So the best among them—Gandalf the wizard, Galadriel the elven queen, and Aragorn the true king—simply refuse to seize the ring, though they have chances, because they recognize their own weakness and their susceptibility to corruption. They choose to live in weakness and humility, even to suffer defeat if they must, rather than risk the corruption that the power of the ring would cause. Ironically, this is what makes them so powerful.

Still, the temptation they face to use the power of the ring, even for a supposedly good purpose, is almost too much to overcome. What tempts the best among them, like Gandalf, is the desire to use the ring to accomplish good. It is power for the sake of showing pity that becomes the real danger because, however well intentioned, the power of the ring would still worm its way into the heart and turn it toward evil. At one point Frodo, a Hobbit and keeper of the ring, says to Gandalf, a great and good wizard, "You are wise and powerful. Will you not take the Ring?" Gandalf replies:

> "No! With that power I should have power too great and terrible. And over me the Ring would gain a power still greater and more deadly. . . . Yet the way of the Ring to my heart is by pity, pity for weakness and the desire of strength to do good. Do not tempt me! I dare not take it, not even to keep it safe, unused. The wish to wield it would be too great for my strength."[4]

Ironically, it is Frodo, the "Halfling," a creature who has no ambition for greatness and wants nothing more than to live a quiet, peaceable life, who is commissioned to take the Ring to Mount Doom in the land of Mordor, where it can be destroyed. Frodo is humble and powerless, which qualifies him to carry out the mission because he is the least likely to use the power of the Ring, even to help others.

I am not suggesting that prayer is like that ring, inherently evil. Frodo was commissioned to destroy the ring because it was corrupt, however good the motives of those who tried to use it. It is hardly the case that prayer is corrupt in the same way. Still, there is something dangerous about prayer. Or better to say, there is something dangerous about us once we receive answers to prayer. God answers prayer for our own good and for his glory. But what we could do with those answers to prayer might turn into something quite different.

Spiritual power is greater than all other kinds of power because it comes directly from God. It is mightier than armies and education and office and wealth. It is the power that created the world, that sustains the world, that redeems the world. It is the power that can heal the blind and raise people from the dead. It is the power that can transform the human heart. There is no power as wonderful and good as spiritual power. It is for that very reason that it is so terrible and dangerous, not because of what God does with it but because of what we might do. God is merciful to us when he does not grant us such power on a whim or wish.

THE ABUSIVE POWER OF PRAYER

Like all other means to power, prayer too is subject to abuse. Our prayers can become selfish and mean and petty. God therefore shows us mercy by not answering all our prayers. If God did answer all our prayers, we would become corrupt beyond measure, praying as if prayer was like a credit card with no limits. We claim, of course, that we would use it for a good purpose and thus pray for noble things. We can make such a claim because it is only that—a claim, an ideal, a theoretical assertion. It is easy to boast of what our prayers would accomplish when so many of our prayers accomplish little or nothing.

But if our prayers were answered—not some of them but *all* of them, especially our very best and worthiest prayers—we would become monsters, far worse than Hitler or Stalin. At first we would be silly, like a little boy showing off a new toy that's the envy of the neighborhood. We would make trees fly in the air, drive our Volvos across the Mississippi, and turn the moon into green cheese.

Then we would become more serious, even noble. The exigencies of life would force us to it. We would pray to God because we had nowhere else to turn and no one else to turn to. We would pray for something we desperately needed or wanted, knowing that an answer from God was our last option. We would pray as I did, so many years ago, asking God to spare the lives of my broken and dying family members after that horrible accident.

What if God had answered that prayer for healing, perhaps the most sincere and desperate prayer I have ever prayed? What if God had instantaneously healed my wife, Lynda, my daughter Diana Jane, and my mother, Grace, right on the spot, dazzling everyone—not only the witnesses on the scene but also everyone else who would hear about it? What would have happened? I can only speculate.

Certainly people would have been shocked and curious. The incident would have received attention from around the world. Newspapers would have covered it for days. Photos of my family would have appeared on the cover of major magazines, and television news programs and talk shows would have clamored to interview us. We would have been given incredible opportunities to witness to our faith and to glorify God.

Perhaps I would have been motivated to do nothing more than to help others and to honor God, at least initially. Perhaps my ministry would have started out that innocently. But it would not have stayed that way for long. Eventually I would have become an expert on prayer and a medium of the miraculous between God and everyone else. I would have been forced to hire an agent and a staff. I would have written a book on prayer (with a very different title from the title of this book!), attracted a following, and started an organization called "Miracle Ministries." I would have held prayer crusades around the world, helping people tap into God's healing power. I would have become famous, powerful, and rich.

Isn't this how it usually works? Isn't this how corruption takes root? God does something extraordinary, like healing family members catastrophically injured in an accident. We want others to experience the same blessing. So we market the miraculous, turn prayer into a technique anyone can master, and win the acclaim of the world. Am I being cynical about human nature? Some programs on religious television remind me that my sober analysis of human nature is not far from the mark.

If God answered all our prayers, sooner or later we would use prayer to advance our own interests and to win the world's acclaim. We would become, as James warned, a friend of the world and thus an enemy of God.[5] We would use the power of prayer simply to gain more power for ourselves until only God stood in our way.

And then we would challenge even God. We would become like the devil himself—pompous, proud, and audacious—using prayer as a means of exalting ourselves, showing off, and taking God's place. Isn't that what Adam and Eve tried to do before they were driven out of the Garden of Eden? Isn't that what the devil tried to do before he was driven out of heaven?

In short, we would use the power of prayer for our own benefit (such as health and wealth, success, and domination) rather than for the good things God wants for us (such as holiness of life, faithfulness in service, and goodness of heart)—even if our initial prayers were desperate and our initial intentions innocent. This all sounds fanciful, I know. But it is not. It is no joking matter. We think we would be exceptions to the rule. But such would never be the case. Spiritual power would intoxicate and corrupt us. The results would be disastrous.

PROTECTION FROM OURSELVES

Is there any exception to the rule? I can think of only one. Jesus himself was aware of the danger of spiritual power. Of all people who could have justified having and using spiritual power, Jesus was surely the one. He waited thirty years before his ministry commenced. His life during those years was so ordinary that we know little about it. There was nothing much to report. He worked as a carpenter, perhaps helped to raise his younger siblings, and meditated on the Torah.

Those years of responsibility, solitude, and obscurity prepared him for the three short years of his public ministry. He began that ministry shortly after John baptized him, the Holy Spirit descended upon him, and his Father in heaven affirmed him as his Son. One would think that Jesus was ready for service by then; he had been seasoned, baptized, affirmed, and filled.

But first he had to face temptation. So the Holy Spirit drove Jesus into the desert, where he was tempted by the devil. Three times the devil tempted Jesus to abuse spiritual power—to indulge his appetites by turning a stone into bread, to gain power over the world by bowing down to the god of this world, and to impress people by performing a miracle, thus winning their admiration. Jesus had all the reason in the world to yield to these temptations. He was hungry. Why not indulge his appetite? Jesus was heir apparent to the world's throne. Why not take a shortcut and feign allegiance to the devil? Jesus was going to be a miracle-worker anyway. Why not dazzle the crowds, making it easier for them to believe?

But Jesus resisted. It was the wrong place, the wrong time, the wrong circumstances to claim and use such power. What qualified Jesus to use spiritual power so effectively is that he put it aside, refusing to use it to advance his own interests. He chose to suffer deprivation first, allowing himself to be purged and purified and thus prepared for the power he would use after he passed the tests.

Ironically, later on Jesus did receive power, prayed fervently, and exercised tremendous influence. He multiplied five loaves and two fishes to feed five thousand people, after having prayed to his Father in heaven. He performed countless miracles—to show mercy, not to show off. Now he is Lord of the entire universe, though only after facing humiliation, suffering, and death. He refused to take advantage of a power that was rightfully his and to assert himself, though he had every right to. Paul states it so well. Though Jesus was

in very nature God,
*   [he] did not consider equality with God something to*
*   be used to his own advantage;*
rather he made himself nothing
*   by taking the very nature of a servant,*
*   being made in human likeness.*
And being found in appearance as a human being,
*   he humbled himself*
*   by becoming obedient to death—even death on a cross!*[6]

That commitment to humility and sacrifice continued to the end, even though Jesus himself seemed at one point to waver, for an obviously understandable reason. Who wouldn't shrink in utter terror at the thought of such an ignominious death? In the Garden of Gethsemane Jesus prayed, "My Father, if it is possible, may this cup be taken from me." That was his prayer, though he added, "Yet not as I will, but as you will."[7] Obviously his prayer was not answered—for our sake, not for his. Imagine if Jesus' prayer had been answered! His life would have been spared, ours doomed. Jesus deserved to have his prayer answered, too. God was merciful, not to Jesus but to us, by refusing to answer the prayer of his own perfect and innocent Son.

> *Unanswered prayer breaks us, seasons us, and refines us so that, in the end, we attain greater spiritual depth and greater spiritual power.*

We are not dealing here with conventional mathematics applied to the spiritual life. According to the Bible, death leads to life, loss to gain, weakness to strength, and suffering to power. Unanswered prayer breaks us, seasons us, and refines us so that, in the end, we attain greater spiritual depth and greater spiritual power.

I am reminded once again of another line in Tolstoy's short story, "Prayer." Mary explains to the mother who has just lost her son:

> "Sometimes it happens like this: Without being guilty of anything, a family can become bankrupt, lose their business, and, instead of a good apartment, live in some dirty room. They don't even have money to buy tea! They all weep, praying for some kind of help. God could satisfy all of their prayers, but he knows that it wouldn't be good for them. They don't see it, but the Father knows that if they lived in luxury with lots of money, they would become completely spoiled."[8]

Hannah Whitall Smith, a nineteenth-century Quaker born and raised in the United States, faced much suffering in her life, though she was an extraordinary woman of influence and prayer. Smith lost four of her seven children. Later, after moving to England, she had to raise two of her grandchildren as well. In her old age she was disabled with rheumatism and spent time in a wheelchair. Yet she relished life, enjoyed God, and loved the people around her. Her grandchildren in particular remembered her romping with them with unbridled enthusiasm. She shared her insights about the Christian faith in *The Christian's Secret of a Happy Life*, which, in addition to imparting practical wisdom about Christian living, contains many prayers.

The unanswered prayers resulting in suffering did not turn Smith away from prayer; it drove her deeper into prayer. "It has been well said that 'earthly cares are a heavenly discipline.' But they are even something better than discipline—they are God's chariots, sent to take the soul to its high places of triumph. They do not look like chariots. They look instead like enemies, sufferings, trials, defeats, misunderstandings, disappointments, unkindness."9

Strange as it may sound, we need unanswered prayer. It is God's gift to us because it protects us from ourselves. If all our prayers were answered, we would only abuse the power. We would use prayer to change the world to our liking, and it would become hell on earth. Like spoiled children with too many toys and too much money, we would only grab for more. We would pray for victory at the expense of others; we would be intoxicated by the power we would wield. We would hurt other people and exalt ourselves.

> *Strange as it may sound, we need unanswered prayer. It is God's gift to us because it protects us from ourselves.*

Unanswered prayer protects us. It breaks us, deepens us, exposes us, and transforms us. Ironically, the unanswered prayers of the past, which so often leave us feeling hurt, abandoned, and disillusioned, serve as a refiner's fire that prepares us for the answered prayers of the future, if we are willing to look deep into the darkness of our own souls and persist in prayer when there doesn't seem to be any reason to.

QUESTIONS FOR DISCUSSION

1. Think of some examples from your past in which it was good that a prayer was *not* answered—that such unanswered prayer was a gift to you.

2. Explore the reasons why prayer for victory can be justifiable. Consider when such prayers might still be wrong. Cite some examples.

3. How can the power of prayer be a dangerous thing? Give some examples.

4. Why were the temptations Jesus faced in the desert so dangerous? How did he resist them?

CHAPTER 5

PRAYER EXCAVATES
THE HEART

Prayer requires more of the heart than the tongue.
ADAM CLARKE (1762–1832)

THE FIRST PASSAGE I MEMORIZED AS AN ADULT CHRISTIAN WAS
Psalm 139. I was in my first year of seminary, very young, a newly
wed, and uncertain about who I was and where I was going. I felt
dissatisfied with life and disquieted by the vague feeling that life
had not turned out the way I wanted, though I was unsure of how
it could be different. I prayed often for release from the burden,
but no release came. I had no obvious reason for complaint either.
The circumstances of my life were safe and secure, yet I felt lost all
the same.

A friend of mine suggested that I meditate on Psalm 139. This
was the first time I had been challenged to memorize an entire text.
His suggestion seemed so demanding that he might as well have told
me to memorize the entire Bible. But I figured that memorizing sec-
tions of the Bible was the kind of thing people in seminary ought to
be doing. So I took up the challenge. It changed my life.

The Psalmist begins by acknowledging that God knows him better than he knows himself.

O LORD, you have searched me
and you know me.
You know when I sit down and when I rise;
you perceive my thoughts from far away.
You discern my going out and my lying down,
you are familiar with all my ways.

He also realizes that he cannot escape the presence of God. God is with him wherever he goes, no matter how hard he tries to escape.

Where can I go from your Spirit?
Where can I flee from your presence?
If I go up to the heavens, you are there;
if I make my bed in the depths, you are there.

In fact, he discovers that God has been with him from the beginning, even before he was conceived. God has designed his appearance and determined the number of his years.

Overwhelmed by this knowledge, the Psalmist surrenders himself to this inescapable, creative, personal God. He wants God to shine light into his soul—exposing him, testing him, purging him, and purifying him. He invites God to have his own way in his life.

Search me, O God, and know my heart;
test me and know my anxious thoughts.
See if there is any offensive way in me,
and lead me in the way everlasting.

SELF-REFLECTION

Psalm 139 introduced me to the discipline of self-reflection. I began to ask God to search my heart as he searched the Psalmist's. Through meditating on Psalm 139 I learned that the greatest burden I had to bear was myself—my selfishness, discontentment, and bad habits. I wanted to cast that burden on God.

Nineteenth-century spiritual writer Hannah Whitall Smith understood this problem so well. She wrote:

> When I speak of burdens, I mean everything that troubles us, whether spiritual or temporal. I mean, first of all, ourselves. The greatest burden we have to carry in life is self; the most difficult thing we have to manage is self. . . . In laying off your burdens, therefore, the first one you must get rid of is yourself.[1]

Self-reflection does not come naturally or easily. There is something in us that resists it. Unlike children, we seem to be more afraid of light than of darkness. It usually takes difficult circumstances— conflicts in relationships, failure at school or at work, inner turmoil— to force us to return to it. It seems that we have to experience darkness for the horror it is, especially the darkness in our own souls, before we are willing to seek the light.

Unanswered prayer is one of those circumstances. It challenges us to explore the deepest places within us and to ask ourselves searching questions. Does the problem lie with God? Or with us? Unable to answer such a question on our own, we pray (if we dare!), "Search me, O God, and know my heart; test me and know my anxious thoughts."

CRAVINGS

Sometimes we read the right book at just the right time, and it changes our lives. I first read *The Confessions* of St. Augustine when I was in my thirties. I read it again when I was forty-five. It was like reading a different book. I inhaled it. I wrote so many comments in the margins that it seemed as if I was writing another book in response to it. I could only read five to ten pages at a time. Then I would have to stop, too stimulated and exhausted to continue. I spent hours meditating on it.

Augustine lived in the fourth century and wrote his *Confessions* in the form of a prayer to God. It is an extended reflection on his long and tumultuous journey to faith. As a precocious teenager, he rejected the Christian faith as too foolish, crude, and repressive to take seriously. He spent the next fifteen years exploring alternatives that appeared to make better sense of the world, especially when it came to explaining the problem of evil. He also indulged his voracious hunger for pleasure and embraced all that the world had to offer. He became a prisoner to his own appetites.

Augustine attended school in Carthage, then the greatest city of North Africa. After completing his studies he moved to Rome, where he taught rhetoric. He ended up in Milan. There he encountered the man who changed his life—Ambrose, bishop of the church in Milan. By then Augustine was beginning to take a fresh look at Christianity. Sunday after Sunday Ambrose's sermons captivated Augustine and eliminated his intellectual objections to the Christian faith. Ambrose persuaded Augustine to believe that the Christian faith was really true, in an absolute sense, far superior to the alternatives he had flirted with.

Still, Augustine would not become a Christian. Something held him back, something hidden deep within. It was the problem of his divided will. On the one hand, Augustine wanted to believe, for he knew that the Christian faith was true and trustworthy. On the other hand, Augustine refused to believe because he realized that he would have to surrender his life to God, which implied giving up the bad habits that had gratified him for so long. He wrote agonizingly of this conflict, wanting both purity and sexual gratification, "Grant me chastity and self-control, but please not yet!"[2] He desired God and aspired to live for God, but he was unwilling to yield his entire self to God.

Augustine became immobilized by the inner conflict. Speaking of his hesitation to become a Christian, he wrote in *The Confessions,* "I ached for a like change myself, for it was no iron chain imposed by anyone else that fettered me, but the iron of my own will. The enemy had my power of willing in his clutches, and from it had forged a chain to bind me."[3] It was only after enduring a period of internal tumult that he surrendered himself to God.

Our cravings can undermine successful prayer because they make us duplicitous. We desire to know God, which is why we pray; but we also crave sin, which separates us from God. Our duplicity makes us insincere, for even while we pray to God, we cherish sin in our hearts. We have, as Augustine put it, a *divided will*.

Harry Emerson Fosdick commented on the same problem in his well-known book on prayer. Our prayers, he said, are not altogether real because they do not represent what we desire in the deepest places in our lives. "We ask God for the 'greater gifts' which we do not desire earnestly. For example, we pray against some evil habit in our lives, while at the same time we refuse to give up the practices that make the habit easy, or the companionships in which the habit thrives."[4]

Unanswered prayer sometimes exposes us for the hypocrites we are. We pray, "O Lord, make me holy," though we refuse to give up a bad habit. Or we say, "O Lord, save this marriage," when we feel nothing but contempt for our husband or wife. We pray for purity of heart while we indulge our appetite for lust, or we pray for humility while we fantasize how we will achieve recognition and glory. Our motives are often mixed and contradictory. Selfishness and impurity plague us, even when we pray. We aren't quite willing to let the sin go. It is enough to drive us mad. I can't imagine what it does to God.

Two cravings in particular come to mind, both of which are destructive to our prayer life. The first craving is our desire for pleasure. We want to indulge our appetite for food, alcohol, and sex, for attention, and for entertainment. A college student becomes addicted to Internet pornography. An adolescent female craves the attention of young males in her high school and almost starves herself to get noticed. A group of men saturate themselves with alcohol on a fishing trip. A young mother keeps the TV going six hours a day.

The second problem is the desire for material wealth and prosperity. A businessman scrambles for professional success, even at the expense of his family. A young professor compromises her convictions to make it big in higher education. It is, as C. S. Lewis noted, the great sin of middle-aged people in particular.[5] We want to make this world our home, which is an old-fashioned way of saying that we want more money, a nicer home, a newer car, a better stereo, a fatter portfolio, a bigger savings account, and greater security.

These cravings affect how we pray. Prayer can reinforce the very habits that need to be broken. We pray for pleasure, for success, for wealth, for comfort—as if prayer itself was intended to indulge our appetite to have more of everything. We don't pray for bread any more; we pray for a lavish banquet. We don't pray for God's kingdom to come; we ask God for our own. We use prayer to feed our cravings. James writes, "You do not have because you do not ask God. When you ask, you do not receive, because you ask with wrong motives, that you may spend what you get on your pleasures."[6]

This approach to prayer may explain why our prayers go unanswered. We are praying for the wrong things.

Still, must we become perfectly pure and holy before we can pray with any degree of success? That seems an impossible goal to reach. Besides, if we did reach it, we would no longer feel the need to pray, so self-satisfied would we be. Perfection, then, is not the solution. It is beside the point. Even if we attained it, perfection wouldn't obligate God to answer our prayers any more than hard work on the job obligates the boss to give us a huge pay raise.

The Psalmist tells us to "see if there is any offensive way" in us because he knows wickedness lurks in his soul, like a predator hidden in the shadows. He cries out to God, very much aware of his own weakness and fallibility. He turns the problem of his own duplicity into a prayer. Searching himself, he asks that God purge and purify him. Rather than drive him away from God, his cravings and failures drive him toward God.

Instead of trying to subdue our cravings *before* we pray, we can turn our cravings into a prayer—into a prayer of confession. How?

By admitting to God that when we pray, we are not always sincere; that when we ask God to help us overcome sin, we are not always genuine because we enjoy sin so much; that when we pray for others in need, we are not always honest because we think far too often about ourselves. When Augustine wrestled with the problem of his own divided will, he admitted that he had a problem and sought God for help. He asked God to overcome his duplicity and make him whole and pure.

> *Instead of trying to subdue our cravings before we pray, we can turn our cravings into a prayer— into a prayer of confession.*

GRUDGES

The habit of craving sin is one reason why our prayers might go unanswered. A second is that we harbor a grudge. In the Lord's Prayer Jesus said, "Forgive us our debts as we forgive our debtors." This condition strikes me as impossibly demanding. We must forgive before we are forgiven? Overcome grudges before our prayers are heard or answered? If anyone has ever held a grudge, he or she knows how hard it is to conquer.

But I think the text means something far different. It doesn't imply that we must make ourselves worthy of forgiveness; instead, it implies that we must simply recognize what sinners we already are. People who forgive understand the frailty and fallenness of their own natures; they are aware of their own desperate need for grace. Consequently, they are willing to forgive others who share the same nature with them, to give to others what they need from God. They forgive because they know they need forgiveness. In their brokenness, whether caused by the cruelty of others or brought on by their own foolish choices, they are ready and willing to receive God's mercy.

Jesus made this point, and in dramatic fashion. An intimate group of friends was dining at the home of a wealthy friend, Simon.

They were reclining around a large table in a central courtyard. Many servants were coming and going. Jesus was there too, a novelty among the guests. The conversation seemed strained and unnatural at first. But Simon's guests soon began to relax and talk among themselves. Simon was relieved, feeling that he would be able to survive the evening.

Suddenly he noticed a woman kneeling at the feet of Jesus. She was wearing suggestive clothing and heavy make-up, a parody of seduction. Her face looked old and haggard, though Simon guessed her age to be no more than twenty-five. She was crying quietly. Her tears fell on Jesus' feet. She dried his feet with her long, black hair. Then she poured perfume on his feet and rubbed it in.

Simon wondered how she had slipped in. He wanted to throw her out but hesitated, largely because Jesus looked completely comfortable. Simon's face grew flush with embarrassment. He didn't know what to do. By then everyone had stopped talking and was staring at Jesus, frozen by the strangeness of the scene. An awkward silence fell over the table. They knew what kind of woman she was; they waited for Simon to act.

Finally Jesus spoke, not to the woman but to Simon, his host. He told Simon a story. There was a man, Jesus said, who had two debtors. One owed him a mere fifty dollars, the other five hundred dollars. Neither had the money to pay off the debt. So the man decided to cancel both their debts out of the goodness of his heart. Jesus then asked Simon, "Which do you think will love him more?" Simon responded, "Obviously the man who owed the greater debt." Jesus told Simon he was right.

Then Jesus turned his head and looked directly at the woman, though he continued to speak to Simon. He told Simon that when he entered his home, no one followed the usual customs of hospitality— like washing his feet and anointing his head with oil. But this woman off the street washed his feet with her tears, wiped them with her hair, and anointed them with perfume. She was the one who owed the greater debt; Simon was the one who owed the lesser debt. She knew her need, far more than Simon did. Jesus canceled her debt. That's why she treated Jesus with great love and respect. The one who is forgiven much loves much, while the one who is forgiven little loves little.[7]

It is easy to spot unforgiving people. They leave a trail of evidence everywhere. They take offense easily and often, and they caress hurts that sometimes go back years, even to childhood. They rehearse the wrongs done to them as if reciting a script. They are absolutely convinced that they were—and are—victims. And rightly so. There are victims in this world, too many of them. Murder, rape, extortion, slander, abuse, and a host of other unspeakable wrongs leave profound and irreversible hurt in their wake.

Victims have a right to withhold forgiveness and to punish the wrongdoer as well, and with good reason. No one can dispute the claim and the charge. But it is unforgiveness, and not only the offense itself, that can cause so much damage, like fallout from a nuclear bomb. Unforgiving people become so preoccupied with the wrong done *to* them—which may be and often is severe and painful—that they cannot see the wrong *in* them. Obsessed by their own pain, they become oblivious to the pain that they inflict on others—on their children, their spouses, their friends, even God.

I was forced to wrestle with this issue after the accident. The drunken driver responsible for the accident was arrested and charged with multiple counts of vehicular homicide. But he was acquitted on a technicality. After the trial I spent months pondering the accident and plotting revenge. I knew my soul was at risk; I realized my anger could turn to poison.

A moment of enlightenment occurred to me when I realized that what separated the driver from me was pure chance—or better, pure grace. While he had grown up in a miserable environment, saturated with abuse, alcohol, and neglect, I had grown up in a relatively healthy environment and had been given opportunities, privileges, and support that, for reasons only God knows, had been denied to him.

Was I inherently better than this man? I don't think so. Was I capable of doing the same thing? I'm sure of it. In choosing to forgive him, I was affirming that we shared a similar nature and a similar need, that we were both sinners in need of grace. Our differences were as much the result of environment, opportunity, and influence as they were of anything else. At that moment I realized that we were no different from each other, not at the core of our being.

Grudges create the same difficulty as cravings do. They make our prayers insincere, and, like cravings, they are extremely hard to overcome. Grudges cause us to obsess about what others have done to us, which keeps us from seeing our own faults and needs. They hold us in their power. If we have to overcome our grudges before our prayers can be answered, then we will rarely see answers to prayer.

There is only one way out of this prison. It is to turn the problem of grudges into a prayer, asking God to do what seems impossible to us, which is to help us forgive those who have hurt us. Once again, our struggles create an opportunity for prayer.

DOUBT

Prayer requires faith. But how much faith? I have prayed for many years and for many things. There have been times when I have approached God with boldness and prayed with the confidence of a young child asking his mother for something as simple as a glass of milk. But not always. There have been other times when I have been plagued with doubt, uncertain of the worthiness of my request or of God's willingness to answer. Is perfect faith required for our prayers to be answered?

The story of Bartimaeus, a blind beggar, asks the same question. Sitting at the outskirts of Jericho, he heard that Jesus was walking by, surrounded by a huge crowd. He cried out, "Jesus, Son of David, have mercy on me!" People tried to quiet him down, assuming that Jesus would be offended by his rudeness, but he persisted.

Jesus finally took notice of the man and stopped, asking him, "What do you want me to do for you?"

Bartimaeus replied, "Rabbi, I want to see." And Jesus restored his sight, right on the spot.

The punch line to the story underscores the importance of faith: "Go; your faith has healed you."[8] It appears that Bartimaeus's faith allowed Jesus to perform the miracle. If there had been no faith, there would have been no healing.

Yet the Bible is not as clear as it would seem. There are other stories of people who approached Jesus with imperfect faith. They had enough faith to ask Jesus for help, but not enough to believe that Jesus would do it. Somehow their prayers were heard, in spite of—or perhaps because of—their lack of pure faith.

Jesus encountered a man who had anything but perfect faith. We don't even know his name. He was deeply distressed because his son suffered from constant seizures. He wanted his son healed. He approached the disciples of Jesus first because Jesus was absent (ironically, he was off praying). The disciples tried to heal his son but failed. When Jesus returned and heard of their failures, he was upset because they lacked faith. "You unbelieving generation," he said. "How long shall I stay with you? How long shall I put up with you?"

Then Jesus asked to see the boy. Immediately the boy had another seizure, fell to the ground, and foamed at the mouth. In a panic the father said to Jesus, "If you can do anything, take pity on us and help us."

Jesus seemed almost offended, "'If you can'? . . . Everything is possible for one who believes."

Immediately the father cried out, "I do believe; help me overcome my unbelief!"[9] Jesus rebuked the spirit that had been controlling the boy, and the boy was healed, just like that.

This father had imperfect faith. It was faith tinged with doubt, faith fighting doubt, faith hoping for a miracle in the face of doubt. True, faith is a condition for answered prayer. But how much faith?

Must it be absolutely perfect and pure? Must we believe beyond a shadow of a doubt? Must we believe that God will, that God must, answer our prayer before we receive any answers?

True, faith is a condition for answered prayer. But how much faith? Must it be absolutely perfect and pure?

Friends of mine received a call several years ago that their son had been injured in a freak accident. While wrestling with friends in a park, their son had broken his neck. He was paralyzed from the neck down. After he underwent a battery of tests, his parents received the bad news. Their son was a quadriplegic.

But this couple would not accept the diagnosis. They believed that God would heal their son; they were sure of it. So they prayed. Their son began to recover in the following weeks and months. Today he shows little evidence of the injury. They prayed in faith, and they received.

But other friends of mine had a daughter who was diagnosed with cancer. They prayed, too, believing with certainty that God could and would heal her. Relying on the advice of physicians who prescribed a certain protocol of treatment for her to follow, they continued to believe that she would be healed. She died.

Did the one couple have enough faith and the other couple not?

Some think so. Most question it. All wonder, "Why one and not the other?" I am aware of spiritual gurus who argue that, if we have true faith, we can and will receive anything we ask for. They defend this point of view logically. Surely God wants us to live happily, to enjoy good health, and to experience the bounty of life. If we lack these things, it is because we do not ask or, if we do ask, we do not ask in faith and thus do not receive. Genuine faith claims and receives God's promises. So if a loved one doesn't get well, it demonstrates lack of faith; if a man or woman can't find work, it indicates lack of faith; if a church fails to grow, it reflects lack of faith. Faith is the key that opens the door to God's miracle-working power.

There is something attractive about this way of thinking. It is so clean and clear. It appeals to our legitimate desire to have the universe operate according to predictable and reliable rules. If we believe, life will go well for us; if we don't, life will be miserable. This viewpoint assumes that God wants to make life good for us, a kind of heaven on earth. It explains why some people enjoy the good life and others don't. The former have enough faith; the latter don't. God wants to give; faith claims the gift. With enough faith, all will be well. It seems so simple.

Perhaps too simple. For one thing, the premise itself is faulty. God has never promised that life on earth was meant to be easy, convenient, and prosperous. Most of the great saints did not experience this kind of prosperity. The apostles, for example, suffered significant loss because of their faith in Christ. All but one died unnatural deaths at the hands of their persecutors. In the book of Hebrews, the unknown author tells the stories of many "heroes" of the faith. Some worked miracles because of their faith, while others suffered greatly because of their faith. Yet *all* received commendation for having genuine faith.[10]

For another, the pressure put on us to muster enough faith is probably more than most of us can bear. It strikes me as cruel to say to the couple who lost their daughter to cancer that she died because they lacked enough faith, just as it strikes me as presumptuous to say to the couple whose quadriplegic son walked again that he recovered because they had enough faith.

John Calvin bristled at the thought that anyone's faith could be that perfect. Not even the saints had perfect faith. Perfect faith is not, nor ever has been, the point. "It is clear the faith of the saints was often so mixed and troubled with doubts that in believing and hoping they yet betrayed some want of faith." So what do we do if we know that we lack perfect faith? Calvin urges us to persist. Perfection is not required—only desire, persistence, and progress. "Although not freed of all hindrances, their efforts still please God and their petitions are approved, provided they endeavor and strive toward a goal not immediately attainable."[11]

Jesus taught that just a little bit of faith—faith the size of a mustard seed—is all we need, which is his way of saying that quantity is not really the point. Only a little bit of faith is necessary so long as it is directed toward the right object, that is, toward God. In fact, faith is not really the main point. What matters is whom we place our faith in. Once we try to quantify faith, we misunderstand its nature.

Faith is not like a stack of bargaining chips that we use in our relationship with God—if we have enough chips, we can pretty much force God to do whatever we want.

Faith is not like a stack of bargaining chips that we use in our relationship with God—if we have enough chips, we can pretty much force God to do whatever we want. Faith turns away from self and comes empty-handed to God. Faith doesn't believe in itself; it believes in God. It doesn't try to manufacture confidence in itself; instead, it turns to God. Faith implies that we bring nothing to God; it asks everything from God.

Ironically, when there is no reason for doubt, there is probably little reason for prayer. Sometimes we pray out of desperation, as we have already discovered. Circumstances force us to it. We have no choice but to pray. But those circumstances, hard as they are, engender doubt as well, either of God or of ourselves, which keeps us from praying. I never had to pray more than after I lost three precious members of my family in the accident, but I never had more doubt either. My need drove me to prayer; my doubt kept me from it. I sat by the hour in a state of frozenness, wanting to pray and yet unable to pray.

The worst thing we can do in the face of doubt is to stop praying, assuming—wrongly, I believe—that only people with perfect faith can pray. We must dare to pray even as we doubt, just as the desperate father cried, "I do believe; help me overcome my unbelief!" True faith is like a light that begins to flicker, however faintly, in the darkness of an experience that beckons us to pray even when we can hardly find the faith to pray.

Many of the great saints through history advise us not to fight darkness but to surrender to it and somehow, *by faith*, find God in that darkness. Jean-Pierre de Caussade, a spiritual director and writer who lived in the seventeenth century, wrote:

> There is no remedy for this darkness but to sink into it. God reveals himself in all things through faith. We are nothing more than blind creatures, invalids as it were, who, ignorant of the virtue of medicines, resent their bitter taste, often imagining they are poison. And all the crises and weakness seem to justify our fears.[12]

THE OPPORTUNITY FOR PRAYER

Once again, the same principle applies, as we saw in the case of cravings and grudges. We must turn doubt into a prayer. We don't need all that much faith in the first place. All we need is faith the size of a mustard seed, just enough to call out to God, even if only in a whisper or a whimper.

Cravings, grudges, and doubts do not have to be enemies of the spiritual life, for they can lead to creative self-reflection. Still, I think we should try to avoid morbid introspection. The line between the two is often blurry. The difference between them depends, in the end, on the goal.

All we need is faith the size of a mustard seed, just enough to call out to God, even if only in a whisper or a whimper.

Creative self-reflection will spur us on to deal honestly with our spiritual problems and to invite God to help us overcome them. It will turn our problems into prayers. Morbid introspection, however, will engender an egoistic preoccupation with our faults and weaknesses. We will feel the pressure to overcome all cravings, grudges, and doubts before we pray. This means, of course, that we will never pray at all.

Soul searching, then, can lead us deeper into God, which is really the point of prayer. If anything, soul searching is a kind of prayer. As the Psalmist prayed, we must ask God to search us and try us and see if there is any evil in us. This prayer by Charles de Foucauld captures precisely what soul searching should accomplish.

> *Father, I abandon myself into your hands.*
> *Do with me whatever you will.*
> *Whatever you may do, I thank you.*
> *I am ready for all, I accept all.*
> *Let only your will be done in me,*
> *and in all your creatures.*
> *Into your hands I commend my spirit.*
> *I offer it to you with all the love that is in my heart.*
> *For I love you, Lord, and so want to give myself,*
> *to surrender myself into your hands,*
> *without reserve and with boundless confidence,*
> *for you are my Father. Amen.*[13]

Still, prayer consists of more than self-reflection. If prayer is confined to that, then it becomes little more than an exercise in self-indulgence. When we pray, after all, we are supposed to be praying *to God*. Moreover, when we pray to God, we are bound, sooner or later, to *ask* God for something. And what if, having done all the creative self-reflection we can, we still find God strangely silent? What if God doesn't answer our prayer, though we have done the best we can to become pure and holy and good? Should we still keep praying?

QUESTIONS FOR DISCUSSION

1. Read Psalm 139. What does it say about human nature? About God's nature?

2. What does it means to ask God to search and test us, and to see if there is any wickedness in us?

3. Make a list of cravings. How do cravings harm the spiritual life?

4. Why are grudges so easy to hold and so hard to overcome?

5. What is required to forgive someone, and what is accomplished by it? Why is it so important?

6. What does it mean to have faith the size of a mustard seed? Can faith be genuine if it isn't perfect?

CHAPTER 6

THE COURAGE TO
KEEP ASKING

He who knows how to overcome with God in prayer
has heaven and earth at his disposal.
C. H. SPURGEON

IT WAS MY SENIOR YEAR OF SEMINARY. I WAS TWENTY-FOUR, LYNDA WAS twenty-five. Married for three years, we decided that it was time to start a family. But no children came, not for nine years. Those years of waiting precipitated a crisis in Lynda's life, even more so than in mine. She ached to be a mother; it was a pain of longing in her soul that would not go away.

We ran the gauntlet of infertility procedures. We tried everything, including surgery. People volunteered all kinds of suggestions, most of them more akin to folk medicine than genuine science. A few of their comments were helpful; most were silly; some were hurtful. But we never gave up the hope of having our own children, though we did eventually begin adoption proceedings.

And we prayed, every day, though for a time Lynda, in utter despair, stopped praying because she felt that God was simply too distant and uncaring. Eventually, at age thirty-four, Lynda conceived and gave birth to Catherine, who was followed in quick succession by David, Diana Jane, and John. After our youngest was born, she told friends in our annual Christmas letter, "If you have been praying that God would give us children, STOP. Your prayers have been answered."

I wish that such stories always ended so happily. But as we all know, they don't. We prayed for nine years before our prayers were answered. At least they *were* answered. I know many couples who prayed with as much faithfulness and expectancy as we did, if not more so. They appeared to be as deserving as we were, if that even matters in the case of prayer. But their prayers were *not* answered.

WHEN SHOULD WE QUIT?

When do we give up, stop asking, quit pushing God to answer us? Sometimes it is obvious. If a woman is praying for a pregnancy and she begins to pass through menopause, there is no reason to continue praying (though we should keep in mind that certain biblical characters, like Sarah and Elizabeth, became pregnant long after it was biologically possible!). If a couple is praying for a sick child and that child dies, there is no reason to continue praying, at least for the healing of the child.

But sometimes it is not so clear cut. Short of something as final as death, how do we know when to stop, when to change our mind, or when to persist? Is there a time limit to prayer, as if prayer functions like a parking meter that runs for a maximum of three hours and then expires? Should we give up after a month of praying, or a year, or perhaps a decade?

Lynda and I discussed this question often. When, if ever, should we have stopped praying for a pregnancy? We were tempted to quit on more than one occasion. But we carried on, day after day, year after year, never failing to ask God for our heart's desire. It became almost monotonous and rote, at least to me, as if I was a phone solicitor, mouthing the same words a hundred or a thousand times a day.

We persisted because we had no reason not to, other than the frustration of feeling that heaven's doors had been slammed shut. I wondered at times whether or not we were annoying God, subjecting him to the spiritual equivalent of Chinese water torture.

So how long should we keep praying? The great masters of prayer have always been clear on this point: We should *persist* in prayer unless and until we have a good reason not to. P. T. Forsyth, a master of prayer, wrote, "Prayer is never rejected so long as we do not cease to pray. The chief failure of prayer is its cessation."[1] An early Christian bishop and writer, Gregory of Nyssa, suggested that persistence in prayer is virtuous. "Moreover, it is necessary for us to persevere in prayer, for prayer is like a leader of a chorus of the virtues."[2] The leaders of the fourteenth-century renewal movement called *Devotio Moderna* taught that persistence in prayer would build confidence that God really does care for us. "We ought to be vigorous in prayer and not easily brought to a halt. Nor should we imagine that God does not want to hear us; rather, even when we feel put off, we should not despair."[3] These voices are a few of literally hundreds who emphasize the same point. When praying, we should keep at it.

The Eastern Orthodox tradition has given us the famous "Jesus Prayer," which provides a method for persistence in prayer. The prayer resulted from a quest to find an answer to the question, "What does it mean to pray 'without ceasing'?" Masters of the spiritual life searched the Scriptures and discovered a prayer that they then used as a spiritual exercise. Repeating the prayer many times each day, the exercise itself would turn prayer into something as natural and rhythmic as breathing.

This prayer is simple and profound: "Jesus Christ, son of God, have mercy on me, a sinner." The most basic concerns that true prayer should address are found in this prayer: It identifies Jesus as God's Son, acknowledges that we are sinners, and asks God for mercy. Repetition of this prayer, which some of the faithful in Eastern

Orthodoxy do up to ten thousand times a day, would enable a novice in the spiritual life to learn to pray unceasingly. It is still another way to persist in prayer.

HOPEFUL RESULTS

I have heard some wonderful stories of the results of persistence in prayer. It is enough to inspire me to keep at it, even when I feel discouraged. A colleague recently told me about a friend who prayed and fasted every Wednesday *for ten years* for the conversion of a neighbor. That neighbor started to attend his church and finally gave his life to Christ. I know a set of parents who prayed for years for a wayward son to return to faith. That son is now in fulltime Christian service. A dear friend appears to have kept her cancerous son alive by praying almost continuously for him for two years now. This mother simply won't take "no" for an answer, not even from God.

But not all prayers are answered, however ardent and frequent they might be. A marriage breaks up, a child remains wayward, a neighbor rejects Christ, a school closes down, a church splits, a recovering alcoholic slips, even though we prayed persistently that it would be different. Disappointment always follows.

In the face of such disappointment, some people give up—sometimes on prayer, sometimes even on God. They simply quit. They stop believing, hoping, and enduring. Unanswered prayer drives them away from God. But other people weather the storm of unanswered prayer and actually emerge from it stronger than before, like a tree overhanging a tempestuous ocean, which is strengthened by its exposure to harsh weather. They become masters of the spiritual life and seasoned practitioners of prayer.

Surprisingly, the people I know who are the most faithful and fruitful masters of prayer are the ones who faced the most devastating experiences of unanswered prayer and yet somehow endured. Their disappointments and failures pushed them deeper into the spiritual life. They learned how to pray with greater power because their prayers seemed at one time to be powerless. What happened to them? What kept them going?

INSTANT RESULTS

Our culture is not our ally here. Occasionally I watch sports with my sons on a Sunday afternoon. During advertisements we switch to other channels. Sometimes we stumble on infomercials. I am always intrigued by the promises made during these infomercials. It is not just the amazing results that are promised, which are bogus enough in themselves. It is the speed with which these amazing results can be—and will be—realized.

Consumers can lose four inches off their waistline *in less than two weeks,* or make a five-figure income per month *within thirty days,* or cook gourmet meals after following only *ten minutes* of instructions. I just had part of my lawn sprayed with hydro-seed. The first question I asked was, "How long before it comes up? How long before I can mow it?" I wanted a beautiful lawn within a week.

Ours is a culture of instant results, instant success, and instant gratification. But "instant" rarely applies to prayer, which is more like planting a tree than sowing a new lawn. It takes time to learn how to pray, to mature in prayer, to see the results of prayer. We can't be in a hurry. It takes a long time for a seedling to become a sturdy tree. Lack of patience and persistence, so common in popular culture, inhibits our growth in the art of prayer.

> *Lack of patience and persistence, so common in popular culture, inhibits our growth in the art of prayer.*

KEEP NAGGING! KEEP KNOCKING!

The New Testament is utterly—and frustratingly—clear at this point. It does not explain unanswered prayer. Instead, it tells us to persist in prayer, though answers do not seem to come. Two parables in particular illustrate the point.

Jesus tells the parable of a widow who had been clearly wronged. Day after day she brought her case before a judge who "neither feared God nor cared what people thought." At first he responded with indifference. Why should he care about the plight of this widow? She meant nothing to him, and her case was insignificant. But then he reconsidered, largely because she kept at him, refusing to take "no" for an answer. He finally relented, saying to himself, "Even though I don't fear God and care what people think, yet because this widow *keeps bothering me,* I will see that she gets justice, so that she won't eventually come and attack me!"

Her persistence, in other words, paid off. She simply wore him down. In the end he succumbed to her requests just to get rid of her.

Jesus does not tell this parable to argue that God is like an insensitive and selfish judge who has to be badgered to respond to our requests. He tells it to teach us that we should be like the widow who persisted in her appeal. The punch line to the parable supports this interpretation. "Listen to what the unjust judge says. And will not God bring about justice for his chosen ones, *who cry out to him day and night?* Will he keep putting them off? I tell you, he will see that they get justice, and quickly."

Finally, Jesus asks a rhetorical question to confront his listeners: "However, when the Son of Man comes, will he find faith on the earth?"[4] Unanswered prayer, then, appears to be a test of faith. We meet that test when we keep praying in spite of the frustration and disappointment we feel when our prayers go unanswered.

A second parable makes the same point. This time Jesus puts his listeners into the story, forcing them to play the key role. Suppose, he says, you have guests who arrive late at night. Caught completely unprepared, you discover that you have nothing to feed them. Your guests are famished. These friends are dear to you, and you want to offer them genuine hospitality. But you cannot find enough food in the house to feed them a simple meal.

So you dash across the street to a neighbor who has a large family and plenty of food on hand. You're nervous, however, because you know your neighbor is irritable and inflexible. You also know he likes to retire early to bed. You don't want to disturb him, yet the needs of your guests outweigh his likes and dislikes. So you knock on his door, first softly and then loudly.

You hear a voice coming from a second floor window.

"Who's there?"

"Your neighbor who lives across the street!" you whisper.

"Are you crazy? It's after midnight. Everyone is fast asleep. But not for long if you keep this up!"

"I just had guests arrive. I have nothing to feed them. I came over to see what you had."

"You should have gone shopping earlier! Now you think to mooch off me? Go somewhere else!"

Your voice becomes agitated, your whispers intense.

"I didn't know they were coming. They just showed up on my doorstep half an hour ago. The grocery store is already closed. If I don't do something, they'll probably leave. Look, I need help."

"I'm going back to bed. I can't believe you're this rude."

You stand in the dark and weigh your options. Should you send your guests to bed hungry? Find a motel room for them? Or knock again, knowing how offended your neighbor will be?

You decide to keep knocking.

A few minutes later your neighbor opens the front door. He looks exhausted and exasperated. He grudgingly lets you in. Refusing to say a word, he signals you to follow him into the kitchen, silently opens the refrigerator and cupboard doors, and then goes back to bed. You raid the cupboards and refrigerator and find ample food. Returning to your home, you have something prepared by the time your guests are finished unpacking and freshening up.

Again, the punch line of the parable is telling. Referring to the irritated neighbor, Jesus says, "I tell you, even though he will not get up and give you the bread because of friendship, yet because of your *shameless audacity [persistence]* he will surely get up and give you as much as you need." Then Jesus concludes the parable with a command, "Ask and it will be given to you; search and you will find; knock and the door will be opened to you."[5]

What kind of God would refuse to answer prayer until or unless he was pressured into it?

Twice over, therefore, Jesus tells us to persist in praying, no matter how long it takes to get an answer.

My rational mind objects. Persistence in prayer is like groveling before God, I think to myself, or like nagging God, as if God were a parsimonious grandfather who has to be badgered into giving his grandson a peppermint buried deep in his pocket. Why should we have to keep asking God for what he knows we need? If we don't need it, no amount of persistence will persuade God to give it anyway. If we do need it, it is odd that we have to ask in the first place. It seems a waste of time and energy. Even worse, it seems to cast a bad light on God.

What kind of God would refuse to answer prayer until or unless he was pressured into it? As a parent, I remind myself almost daily not to succumb to pressure from my kids because it turns them into whiners and nags. Is this what God wants us to become?

PERSISTENCE DRIVES US TO GOD

Still, there may be good reason for persistence in prayer. It can affect us in positive ways. First, persistence drives us to God, again and again, thus reinforcing the relationship. The point of prayer, after all, is the relationship itself, not the things we get from the relationship. Who would respect a son who values his father only because that son gets to use the car? We would call him selfish. We would only respect a son who sees the use of the car as an expression of his father's generosity and who loves his father for it.

I am in the middle of raising three teenagers. My daughter Catherine, now nineteen, has changed significantly over the past year, having just completed her first year of college. I still remember the irritation I felt when, during those middle teen years, she seemed to view me as little more than a source of money, wheels, and food. I'm not sure I was a real person to her back then, someone worth talking with, listening to, and enjoying. Now our relationship is exactly that—a relationship. We go out for lattes, talk about everything under the sun, and appreciate each other. She doesn't ask me for things any more—not nearly as often as she used to anyway. I'm not simply a source for the things she wants; I am a person worth knowing.

Persistence can enrich our relationship with God. Admittedly, unanswered prayer wears down faith and hope. We question God's goodness, love, and generosity, and we doubt whether God is capable or willing to meet our needs. If God doesn't deliver the goods when and how we ask, then why pray at all? Is he really as good as we thought he was?

But the problem is that we view God as the source of the things we want, as if God were a vending machine that is supposed to cough up what we desire if we deposit enough prayers.

Is the purpose of prayer to receive what we ask for? Well, yes and no. God wants to answer our prayers. But God wants us to know him, too. If anything, that is God's best answer to prayer (as we will see later on). Persistence leads to a more mature prayer life. We will begin to see God as worthy of our greatest love and affection, as if a *relationship* with God were the goal of our prayers and not merely the acquisition of things we want from God. We will stop talking all the time, and we will learn to listen. We will begin to enjoy God as God. As Harry Emerson Fosdick writes, "One of our strongest misconceptions concerning prayer is that it consists chiefly in our talking to

God, whereas the best part of prayer is our listening to God."[6] In short, persistence will help us to grow up spiritually.

I am learning that my natural inclination is to use God, not to love God. I am like a spiritual junkie. I want the quick fix that answered prayer can provide. Once I get what I want, I return to my normal state of spiritual indolence. Unanswered prayer can actually serve to fan the flame of spiritual desire to know God as the supreme end in life.

If answers to prayer came too easily, we would lose interest, not only in prayer, but also in God.

I like what John Chrysostom wrote about the benefit of unanswered prayer:

> I prayed for many things and was not heard. For even this occurs often to your advantage. Since [God] realizes that you lost heart and are indolent, and that when you attain what you need you depart and no longer pray, God protects you with the pretext of need so that you may concern yourself with him more closely and devote yourself to prayer.[7]

If answers to prayer came too easily, we would lose interest, not only in prayer but also in God.

PURGING AND PURIFYING

Persistence also purges and purifies us. Unanswered prayer might force us to change *how* we pray, though we keep praying all the same. Far from giving up, our prayers will move us ever closer to the heart of what God wants for us.

Some people persist for years in praying to God for the same thing—the conversion of a parent, the growth of a church, the healing of strife within a family. In the end their prayers get results; they get what they asked for.

Other people persist for years in praying for something that never happens. Instead of giving up, they change how they are praying. They begin to pray that God will help them to love a child who does not return to the faith, to forgive a spouse who does not want reconciliation, to remain faithful to a church that keeps declining.

The apostle Paul serves as a good illustration. Paul had what he called "a thorn in my flesh." He does not tell us what it was—bad eyesight perhaps, or opposition from the Jews, or a specific temptation that would not leave him. We simply do not know. He spoke of it in the gravest of terms. It was a "messenger of Satan," a source of torment, a scourge to him.

Paul asked God three times over to deliver him from the problem, but God didn't answer his prayer. So Paul changed how he was praying. He prayed that God would help him to rely on God's power, which was made perfect in Paul's weakness. "Therefore I will boast all the more gladly about my weaknesses, so that Christ's power may rest on me. That is why, for Christ's sake, I delight in weaknesses, in insults, in hardships, in persecutions, in difficulties. For when I am weak, then I am strong."[8]

Just over a year ago the college at which I teach lost one of its most beloved professors, Howard Gage. He died from complications associated with Parkinson's disease. Several months before his death Howard preached in chapel. He used the story of Paul's thorn in the flesh to talk about his own. Like Paul, he wanted deliverance from his affliction, and so he prayed for it. But God didn't answer his prayer.

So Howard had to learn to live with the disease. In chapel he reflected on the difficulties of having Parkinson's. His dependence on medication turned his life into a roller coaster of ups and down. As he commented, "My wife says that when I'm high on my medicine, I act as if I can leap a tall building in a single bound, and when the medicine drops me, I act as if I could not even get out of a phone booth to look at that tall building." He battled stiffness, lack of coordination, insecurity, and depression. His mood swings and strange behavior made him feel uncomfortable around people because he assumed—sometimes correctly—that other people felt uncomfortable around him.

Though Howard never stopped praying, he did over time begin to pray differently. Rather than pray that his weakness be overcome, he concentrated on God's goodness and strength, which was made perfect in his weakness. He became deeply aware of God's provision in his life. "On the days the medicine is not working, the Lord has to give me a lot of grace. In those times, Christ has been there for me."

Howard recognized the gifts that God had given to him—his faithful and loving wife of thirty-eight years, financial stability, a job he loved, and many loyal friends. But Howard was a gift to us, too. He became the champion of the college's mission, a source of encouragement to all, especially to new faculty, and an example of God's love for the campus.

At Howard's memorial service, which was packed with faculty, students, and alumni, a speaker asked the people who could remember having had a significant encounter with Howard in just the two weeks prior to his death to stand up. An astonishing number of people—as many as 150—rose from their seats, a fitting tribute to a man who had never stopped praying, though his prayers were not answered as he had wanted.

Howard's illness did not keep him from praying. If anything, he learned to pray with greater depth, openness, and patience. He followed advice that Henri Nouwen gives: "You must be patient . . . until your hands are completely open."[9]

PERSISTENCE CHANGES GOD

There is one more thing that persistence can accomplish. We already know that persistence can change us. But it can also change God. Persistent prayer can appeal to God to shape the course of history.

William Carey, a pioneer missionary to India who took unspeakable risks to advance the cause of the Christian faith, never did anything without praying first. He believed that prayer was far more than a pious exercise that would change the person who did the praying. He believed that prayer could alter history. "Without God, we cannot; without us, God will not." In his mind, the "us" referred not only to the work Christians do but also to the prayers Christians utter before God.

Richard Foster writes in his popular book, *Celebration of Discipline,* "We are working with God to determine the future! Certain things will happen in history if we pray rightly. We are to change the world by prayer."[10] When we pray, we are not simply mouthing words, as if we were doing little more than having a conversation with ourselves. We are addressing the almighty God! We are asking him to intervene on someone's behalf. We are requesting that he do something that will change the course of history. If we pray, history will turn out one way; if we don't, it will turn out another way. It seems almost too wild and wonderful to be true, like a fanciful story told by a child given to gross exaggeration.

Why God takes so much time to answer our prayers, if he answers them at all, is another question altogether. It is a mystery. Still, for some reason persistence is necessary. Does God need the badgering? I doubt it. Perhaps *we* need to do the badgering—for our sake. Persistence clarifies our mind, reinforces our determination, and deepens our desire for the things that really matter.

My kids have asked me for many things over the years—a CD player, bicycle, boat, car, house, exotic vacations (New Zealand is the most recent request), the moon for all I know. You name it, they have asked for it. I ignore them most of the time. I am as hardhearted as they come, a parent made of granite. My ears perk up, however, when they persist, because persistence usually means that they are serious about something. They have thought about it and checked their motives. They have good reasons, which they express carefully to me. "Dad, I know a new bicycle is expensive. But I've outgrown my old one, and I'm riding my bicycle more and more. I really think I'm ready for an upgrade." Such persistence is persuasive to me.

God has invited us to help shape the course of history (a topic we will return to later). Perhaps that is what he had in mind from the very beginning when he told Adam and Eve to "have dominion." Most of the time we exercise dominion without thinking much about it. We simply live and love and work, taking little notice of our impact on the larger world. But that doesn't mitigate the impact itself. We leave a mark on the world, whether we want to or not. We affect history simply by doing life, often in ways almost too ordinary to notice. What we do makes a difference, no matter what we do.

We also shape the course of history by how we pray, or fail to pray. Persistent prayer has an impact because it invites God—or better, demands God—to do something important, thus making us like the widow who kept nagging the ruthless judge or the friend who kept knocking on his neighbor's door at midnight.

We must, therefore, keep at it. If our children are wayward, we must pray for their return from the far country. As long as there is injustice, we must pray for justice. When we face conflict, we must never stop praying for reconciliation. Though unanswered prayer will tempt us to quit, we must carry on, refusing to give up. Why I don't know. But for some reason persistence in the end gets results.

GOD'S PERSISTENCE

Perhaps it works because it imitates God's own persistence—with us. No nagging mother, whining child, smothering supervisor, exacting piano teacher, or bossy coach has been or ever will be as persistent as God is. God has been chasing after human beings—relentlessly so—since the fall of Adam and Eve. He wants a relationship with us. Though constantly spurned, he keeps after us, like a suitor who can't take a hint. If anyone won't take "no" for an answer, it is God.

The Old Testament tells one long story of Israel's unfaithfulness and God's persistence. While wandering in the desert, the people of Israel rejected God and worshiped a golden calf, though God was the one who delivered them from slavery in Egypt. After entering the Promised Land, they prostituted themselves to foreign deities, though God was the one who secured the land for them. As they expanded their borders and conquered other nations, they horded wealth, pursued pleasure, and exploited their captives, though God was the one who provided them with abundance.

God never gave up. He warned them and wooed them, like a protective parent who will do anything to keep a wayward child from going off the deep end. He sent plagues to scourge them, foreign armies to punish them, prophets to beg them to return to him. He always welcomed them back, no matter how many times they were unfaithful (though he did not hesitate to discipline them, too). He valued the relationship far more than they did. He was the unrequited lover who refused to give up.

He behaves that way with us, too. In God's eyes, it seems that any kind of relationship he can have with us is better than none at all, however hard and tumultuous the relationship might appear to be. The story of one Old Testament character proves the point. Jacob is one of my favorite characters, an antihero if there ever was one. He was crafty, manipulative, and selfish. He was a schemer who would give a Mafia boss a run for his money. Twice over he cheated his older brother, Esau—first out of his rights as the firstborn of the family and then out of his father's blessing. When someone tried to cheat Jacob, he did his best to get even, and then some.

> *In God's eyes, it seems that any kind of relationship he can have with us is better than none at all, however hard and tumultuous the relationship might appear to be.*

Surprisingly, neither the Old Testament nor the New Testament labels him a moral failure. If anything, he is cited as a model of faith. One incident shows why. After spending many years in a foreign country, Jacob decided to return home. By then he had become rich and powerful. So he packed up his wives and many children, his flocks and herds, and his treasures to make the long journey back to his homeland.

He was terrified, however, because he knew he would have to face his brother Esau, with whom he had never been reconciled, even after all those years. To appease Esau—or perhaps to bribe him—he sent caravans of wealth ahead of him as gifts for Esau. Then he sent his wives and sons. He followed last of all, hoping that by the time Esau saw him, Esau's anger would have been mollified by all those riches.

He had to spend one night alone before meeting Esau. It proved to be the turning point of his life. During the night he had an encounter with some kind of divine being who showed up and—odd as this may sound—started to wrestle with Jacob. Why we don't know. The text gives no reason. They fought most of the night because Jacob refused to be defeated. He was as tenacious as a kid brother who refuses to say "uncle."

The divine being finally seized the advantage by putting Jacob's leg out of joint, which caused Jacob to limp for the rest of his life. Then he gave Jacob a new name, "Israel." It is a peculiar name, and not particularly complimentary. Yet the name reflects a quality of character that God values. It literally means, "one who strives with God." Jacob was a fighter, so that became his name. And not only his name, but also the name of God's chosen people, for all time.

That is what God looks for in us. He wants us to strive with him, as he does with us. To wrestle with him as if our life depended on it, because it probably does. To persist in prayer, no matter how much the odds are stacked against us. To refuse to take "no" for an answer from God, just as God has refused to take "no" for an answer from us, no matter how long and hard we have resisted him. It is the least we can do, what God has done for us, what love requires and prayer demands.

Persistence is a good way to respond to unanswered prayer. In effect, it is saying, "God, you may choose *not* to answer my prayers. But I'm going to keep praying all the same, even if you get sick of it."

Still, it might be wise to think about what we are praying for. After all, we don't want to persist in asking what is clearly contrary to God's desire and design. How can we pray with wisdom and confidence, so that our prayers become more quietly thoughtful than guesses shouted out during a game of charades? We are supposed to persist in prayer. That much is clear. But what should we actually pray persistently about?

QUESTIONS FOR DISCUSSION

1. When have you persisted in prayer? What happened?

2. Have you ever given up praying for something? Why?

3. How do you make sense of the two biblical parables explored in this chapter?

4. What are some reasons for persisting in prayer? Do you find them persuasive? Why or why not?

5. What do you think about Jacob's being a role model of faith? Recount an experience or two when you wrestled with God.

6. What is the significance of saying that God has always been persistent with us? How have you seen evidence of that in your life?

CHAPTER 7

PRAYING ACCORDING TO GOD'S WILL

We have to pray with our eyes on God,
not on the difficulties.
OSWALD CHAMBERS

A FEW YEARS AGO, WHILE RESEARCHING MATERIAL FOR A BOOK I WAS writing on religion and the Second World War, I decided to try to relive the war through the experience of those who were reporting on it, as if I were living through it for the first time. I selected several magazines and newspapers and read them as someone would have who, living back then, was trying to keep up with the news. I started in September of 1939 and concluded in August of 1945. I became a contemporary, an eyewitness, an ordinary citizen who, like everyone else at that time, was caught up in those great events.

This approach to research had a profound effect on me, one I did not expect. Of course I already knew what was going to happen, living over fifty years after the fact. I knew about Pearl Harbor, the atomic blasts that leveled Hiroshima and Nagasaki, and the Holocaust. Yet my imagination was vivid enough when I read these contemporary accounts to thrust me into the story as it was unfolding. It made me uneasy and fearful.

For example, I felt panicked as December 7, 1941 approached, the date the Japanese bombed Pearl Harbor. I wanted to call someone on the telephone and warn them of the imminent disaster. The same thing occurred during the weeks before America dropped the atomic bombs. I wanted to advise the Japanese to surrender so they would be spared the devastation about to overtake them. I felt utterly helpless. There was nothing I could do. The future that loomed ahead when I read the accounts had already become the past, at least to me. I was trapped in a time warp.

I felt the most helpless, however, when I read about the Holocaust. I ran across brief reports about "death camps" and the "final solution" as early as 1942. The very idea seemed so preposterous that few people seemed to take it seriously. The frequency of these reports increased over the next few years, and so of course did the level of alarm and concern.

Most people were incredulous. They dismissed the reports as just so much propaganda, like the reports of German brutality that had surfaced during the First World War, later proven to be bogus. It was simply unthinkable that a civilized nation like Germany—a supposedly Christian nation as well—would attempt to exterminate an entire race of people. Finally the allied armies swept into Germany and liberated the camps. Reports of the carnage trickled out, and photos of corpses piled high as small mountains appeared in newspapers. The public was horrified. As one editorial put it, "So it was true after all!"

Like most people, I would give almost anything to be able to change the course of history so that there would have been no Pearl Harbor, no atomic blasts, and no Holocaust. Knowing what I do now, I would have urged America not to wait until 1941 to enter the war, and I would have advised more aggressive intervention on behalf of the Jews. I would have advocated these actions because I know how things turned out. But I have no power to change what happened. It is already in the past. So, though I witnessed the war almost firsthand, I was a helpless observer, powerless to change a thing. I couldn't even save one life.

Influencing the Future

While history deals with the past, prayer deals with the future. We already know what happened in the past, though we can do nothing to change it. We don't yet know what will happen in the future, though we can do something to influence it. We can shape the future by how we pray and thus create the very history we will someday know as the past.

> *We can shape the future by how we pray and thus create the very history we will someday know as the past.*

It is for this very reason that prayer makes me nervous. I wonder how I should pray, believing as I do that my prayers can make a difference. I want to make bold requests, but I hesitate because I don't want to pray wrongly or foolishly or presumptuously. I assume that prayer has power, that prayer can change the course of history. Yet I am cautious about using that power lest I abuse it and God thus withhold it. Prayer is not a matter that should be taken lightly. It is like handling an explosive.

The New Testament does not err on the side of caution. It makes outrageous promises about prayer. These promises are as clear and direct as the commands of an officer during an important battle.

- "I will do whatever you ask in my name, so that the Father may be glorified in the Son. You may ask me for anything in my name, and I will do it."[1]
- "If you remain in me and my words remain in you, ask whatever you wish, and it will be done for you."[2]
- "Very truly I tell you, my Father will give you whatever you ask in my name. Until now you have not asked for anything in my name. Ask and you will receive, and your joy will be complete."[3]

According to God's Will

But there's a condition attached to the promise, and most of us know what it is, intuitively if not consciously. We know we can't ask God for just anything. We must make reasonable requests. In short, we must pray *according to God's will*. If prayer were a blank check, we would need two signatures to cash it in. One would be our signature; the other would be God's signature. God himself must sign off on our requests. He must give final approval.

This sounds simple enough. But what exactly does it mean to pray "according to God's will"? On one level it seems obvious. Giving it even a moment's thought, I wouldn't have much trouble making a long list of requests that would be worthy of God's attention. At least I wouldn't have to think twice before answering them if I were God! Which sounds glib, I know. Yet who hasn't entertained the same thought when asking God for something that seems right, good, and true? How could God *not* will the conversion of a troubled neighbor, the deliverance of an addicted friend, or the restoration of a broken relationship? It seems like a no-brainer to me.

Yet anyone who has prayed for these things will testify that it doesn't always happen according to plan and prayer. This makes me wonder: What does it really mean to pray according to God's will?[4]

I find some comfort in knowing that even the great saints have wrestled with this issue. Take Martin Luther, for example. Luther spent many years living in a monastery. When he left the monastery and the Roman church, he remained unmarried. His duties were too many and his circumstances too dangerous to entertain the possibility of marriage. He surprised everyone, however, when he decided to marry Katharina von Bora, a former nun. He was forty at the time; she was twenty-six. They had six children together.

One daughter was especially dear to Luther. In September, 1542, their thirteen-year-old, Magdalene, became ill. Luther devoted himself to her care and prayed for her recovery. But she only grew worse. Becoming frightened and bewildered, Luther wondered how he should pray. He was certain about what he wanted, but less certain about what God willed. Hope and longing told him that his desires and God's will were one and the same thing. Still he prayed, "I love her dearly, but if it be thy will, dear God, to take her, I shall be glad to know that she is with thee."

When Magdalene was lying—and dying—in bed, he said to her, "Magdalene, my little daughter, you would gladly remain here with me, your father. Are you also willing to go to your Father in heaven?"

She replied, "Yes, dear father, as God wills."

Luther was tormented. What he wanted as her earthly father clouded his understanding of what God willed as her heavenly Father. "The spirit is willing, but the flesh is weak," he said. "I love her very much. . . . In the last thousand years God has given to no bishop such great gifts as he has given to me. I am angry with myself that I am unable to rejoice from my heart and be thankful to God, although I do at times sing a little hymn and thank God. Whether we live or die, we are the Lord's."[5]

When his daughter drew near to death, he fell on his knees before her bed and, weeping bitterly, prayed that God might save her, if it be his will. A little while later, she died in his arms.

GOD'S REVEALED WILL

Luther never really settled the issue. Nor have the rest of us. What is God's will? And how do we know? Christianity has always made a distinction at this point between God's *revealed* will and God's *hidden* will.[6] God's revealed will refers to what God has communicated clearly to us in Scripture. God has taken the initiative to make his will known, and it is not hard to understand. When I want my children to do something, I make it clear to them. I assign them chores, usually specific chores, complete with deadlines. "Please vacuum the living room, by dinner time." "Mow the lawn before the sun goes down." "Fold the wash, and I need it done right away."

God's Word has that same kind of clarity. John Calvin believed that for us to pray with power, we must first understand who God is and what God has planned. We must therefore study Scripture and so come to know the heart of God. Only then will we be able to pray according to God's will. Otherwise, we pray out of ignorance. "It remains for us to seek in him and in prayers to ask of him, what we have learned to be in him."[7] God has not left us in the dark. He has communicated what we need to know.

Still, I wonder if it is that easy. If there's a problem, I'm not sure that it is lack of knowledge, not entirely anyway. It could be lack of courage and conviction. Do we really *want* to know God's will? This question makes me squirm. I probably know enough already. I know, but I don't necessary believe or do. I want life to be nice, safe, and secure. But, as C. S. Lewis put it, God does not want to make life nice for us because he wants to make us new. That is his will. When we pray, we should keep that end in mind.[8] It is enough to make me think twice about praying at all.

> *I pray with greater caution than I used to. Or, if not with greater caution, then certainly with greater sobriety. I realize what I am in for.*

I pray with greater caution than I used to. Or, if not with greater caution, then certainly with greater sobriety. I realize what I am in for. I strive to read the New Testament with fresh eyes. What is it, I ask, that God wills? Then I try to pray accordingly. I look for passages that reveal what God really wants to accomplish in our lives and in the world. Much of it runs contrary to what our culture values, and to what I value.

The New Testament is frighteningly radical. It talks about becoming peacemakers, enduring persecution, praying for enemies, striving to be poor in spirit, dying to self, and offering ourselves as a living sacrifice to God. Jesus taught that if we want to be his disciples, we must deny ourselves, take up our cross, and follow him.

Perhaps the apostle Paul put it best:

> Therefore, I urge you, brothers and sisters, in view of God's mercy, to offer your bodies as a living sacrifices, holy and pleasing to God—this is your proper worship as rational beings. Do not conform to the pattern of this world, but be transformed by the renewing of your mind. Then you will be able to test and approve what *God's will* is—his good, pleasing, and perfect will.[9]

Is this God's will? Is this what we should pray for? It makes me shudder to think so.

IS SUFFERING THE WILL OF GOD?

What about suffering? Does God's will include even that? I used to recoil from the idea, thinking it was unworthy of God, as if suffering and God's will were complete opposites, the spiritual equivalent of oil and water. I suppose on one level that they are. God does not cause suffering for the sake of suffering itself. He does not delight in human misery as if he were a sadist pushing pins into a doll.

This is no mere academic question to me. I have thought long and hard about it since the accident occurred some eleven years ago. For a long time I could not imagine that the accident was or could be the will of God, on any level. The very idea was utterly repulsive to me.

But now I am not so sure. After all these years I have experienced the fruits of it. I have seen what God has done in me, in my children, and in many others. Though the suffering was bad, the effect has been good. Though the accident contradicted God's good design for our lives (mothers and children are not supposed to be snatched from the home in that way!), it nevertheless served to accomplish God's will, too, largely in the way God used it to transform us, and not only us but thousands of other people as well. I know for certain that God has used the accident to change my life. I am far more patient now, especially at home. I am far more flexible with my time, generous with my resources, and calm when facing turbulence.

In short, suffering has done me good, though I would have never chosen it. Not then, and probably not even now. I'm not sure that we should pray for suffering. Suffering just is, as unavoidable as birth and death. Sooner or later it visits everyone, no matter how rich and powerful that person happens to be. But I do think that we should pray for the good effects that suffering can produce, all by God's grace. If there is another way, then so be it. If not, then let the suffering come. Again, as the apostle Paul wrote when God chose *not* to remove his thorn in the flesh, "That is why, for Christ's sake, I delight in weaknesses, in insults, in hardships, in persecutions, in difficulties. For when I am weak, then I am strong."[10]

This view of God's will turns prayer into a risky venture, and it will probably make us more ambivalent when we pray. Even Jesus was ambivalent, on one occasion at least. It was just before the crucifixion. He was alone, the last time he would be. He wanted to save his life, but he knew that his Father's will was to take it.

The tension between his will and his Father's was almost too much for him. In Gethsemane he asked God to deliver him from his destiny. Was there another way? "Father, if you are willing, take this cup from me." Yet he realized that his Father's will was primary. In the end he submitted himself to it: "Yet not my will, but yours be done."[11] When Jesus left the garden, he was ready for the horror that awaited him. He had surrendered his will to his Father's. In effect, he had said, "Here I am. Make me what you will. Do with me as you will. Put me to whatever test or task you will. I am yours."

PRAYING SCRIPTURE

Whether we want to know—and pray according to—the will of God is one issue; how we actually come to know that will is an altogether different issue, and one far easier to address. We can know God's revealed will through Scripture. Moreover, we can pray according to God's will by studying and using the great prayers of Scripture. The Old Testament contains many such prayers (Hannah's prayer, Esther's prayer, Abraham's prayers), as does the New Testament. These are worth reciting to God. That way, when we pray, we will be assured that we are praying according to the will of God.

I have read these prayers many times. It is startling to consider what they *don't* say. They say nothing about long life, perfect health, or success in the popular sense—nothing, in short, that even hints of a desire for an ideal life on earth, free of problems and difficulties. Instead, these prayers ask God for a deeper experience of his love, for purity of life, for inner strength, and for knowledge to make good choices.

The apostle Paul, for example, wrote several beautiful prayers that show us how to pray according to the revealed will of God. Two prayers come to mind. The church in Philippi was one of Paul's favorites. He had spent only a short time there before being driven out by his Jewish opponents. He left behind a fledgling church only months old. Yet those new believers endured in faith, had great joy, and contributed out of their poverty to help Christians living in Jerusalem. Here is Paul's prayer for them:

> And this is my prayer: that your love may abound more and more in knowledge and depth of insight, so that you may be able to discern what is best and may be pure and blameless for the day of Christ, filled with the fruit of righteousness that comes through Jesus Christ—to the glory and praise of God.[12]

The church in Ephesus faced hardships too. Paul spent nearly three years there. Once again, his prayer reflects what he wanted for them, what he believed God willed for them.

> I pray that out of his glorious riches he may strengthen you with power through his Spirit in your inner being, so that Christ may

dwell in your hearts through faith. And I pray that you, being rooted and established in love, may have power, together with all God's people, to grasp how wide and long and high and deep is the love of Christ, and to know this love that surpasses knowledge—that you may be filled to the measure of all the fullness of God.[13]

GOD'S HIDDEN WILL

There is another dimension, however, to the will of God. The will of God is not just revealed; it is also *hidden*. Unlike the revealed will of God, which can be known through Scripture, the hidden will of God is inscrutable and mysterious. It encompasses God's sovereign control over history, which he is guiding to an unknown but glorious ending. God knows because he transcends time and space; we don't know because we are bound by time and space. God experiences all times as the present; he lives in all places at once. God is sovereign over all; he is in complete control.[14]

Everything that happens somehow fulfills his ultimate will—which is an admittedly hard concept to grasp and to accept. There is so much that has happened in history that seems to contradict what a good God would want. The very idea of a "hidden will" seems odious and offensive. As O. Hallesby, the author of one of the great books on prayer, declares, "No aspect of God becomes a stumbling block to us more easily than His inscrutability."[15]

The Old Testament story of Joseph illustrates the difference between God's revealed will and God's hidden will. Though it has a happy ending, we should not let that happy ending keep us from seeing how harsh and gritty the story is. Clearly what happened to Joseph seems contrary to God's will. If anything, it was the direct result of disobedience to God's revealed will.

In jealousy Joseph's brothers betrayed him and sold him as a slave to a caravan of traders traveling to Egypt. Then, several years later, the wife of his master, Potiphar, betrayed him as well. He spent years in slavery, and still more years in prison, all as an innocent man. Who would dare to call such misery and injustice the will of God?

Yet if it had not been for these horrible events, which ran contrary to God's revealed will, then something worse would have occurred. The people of Egypt would have suffered mass starvation; Joseph's family would have perished, too, long before they became the nation of Israel. Joseph's brothers would not have learned a painful but necessary lesson about justice and loyalty, nor would Joseph have learned about sacrifice and forgiveness. Perhaps God would have worked differently to achieve the same ends. We will never know. What we do know is that God worked mysteriously to accomplish a plan that no eye could see, no mind could understand. It was the hidden, inscrutable will of God.[16]

The cross is the quintessential example of the difference between the two. The people who put Jesus to death were guilty of murder, for Jesus was clearly innocent. What they did violated the revealed will of God, or so everyone thought at the time. Yet the disciples of Jesus eventually changed their mind. They came to believe that God planned and controlled everything. Though Jesus' opponents made a wicked choice by executing Jesus, God accomplished his sovereign purposes all the same.

The early followers of Jesus understood this tension. For example, after suffering persecution, they chose not to flee to safety but to turn to God in prayer. They interpreted their suffering in light of Jesus' suffering. They recognized that Jesus' enemies had promulgated great injustice, but they also believed that God was in control, accomplishing his sovereign purpose. "Indeed Herod and Pontius Pilate met together with the Gentiles and the people of Israel in this city to conspire against your holy servant Jesus, whom you anointed. They did what your power and will had decided beforehand should happen."[17]

No one understood this plan at the time of the crucifixion. It was only later—after the resurrection—that the apostles could look back and recognize that God's hand was in it. They were able to understand the significance of it only in retrospect. Likewise, we won't know the meaning of God's hidden will except by looking back over time and seeing a pattern emerge. What might seem at the time to be senseless, tragic, and meaningless will take on greater significance when we see what happens as a result. Only then will the apparent contradiction between God's revealed will and God's hidden will be resolved.

PRAYING IN THE MIDST OF MYSTERY

The difference between God's revealed will and God's hidden will might seem at first to complicate prayer. What does it mean to pray "according to God's will" when, though we try to pray according to God's revealed will, we see events unfold that seem to contradict it? It could be that God accomplishes his hidden will *through our prayers,* which are based on thoughtful consideration of his revealed will. Perhaps the two are not as contradictory as it would seem.

I recently listened to a radio interview that explored this great mystery better than anything I have heard. The newscaster was interviewing a famous novelist, asking her about a book she was just beginning to write. At one point the novelist said, "I am just getting to know the characters right now. I am becoming friends with them. In fact, I'm irritated by one of them. I can tell that he is going to cause me problems and get himself into trouble. I'm not quite sure what to do about him."

Ironically, she was referring to characters in a novel that she was about to write. Those characters are the product of her mind and imagination. They do not in fact exist at all, except in her own head. She will design the plot and develop the characters before she starts to write. When she is done, the entire novel will be hers, every word of it. Yet she talked about the characters as if they were real. She was just "getting to know them," and she was even angry at one of them because he was making decisions she didn't like. She was left wondering how his life was going to affect the story.

I wonder sometimes if this is how it works. On one level the entire course of history is like a novel that God himself has written. It is his story, his invention, his plan. Being sovereign and transcendent, he is the one who has created the whole thing. It is under his control. Yet on another level the characters he has created are real. They make decisions. They love or hate their enemies, seek God or spurn God, accomplish good or do evil. They even pray. Their actions help to shape the plot that remains, in some mysterious way, under the control of the author.

The analogy is not perfect because the characters in a novel aren't real. But we are real. God has pulled off the amazing feat of writing a story that produced real people who make real decisions that have real consequences. Amazingly, these real people can even pray to the very author who has invented them. Moreover, their prayers will actually shape the very story that they are in. It is all part of a greater whole, which we know as God's hidden will.

Is it possible? It must be, for we have one event in history that captures the essence of this mystery. It is the Incarnation. The more I ponder the Incarnation, the more I am utterly mystified by it. It is a wonder to me, more dazzling than supernovas and more puzzling than the theory of relativity. I can't begin to wrap my mind around it.

Here is a God who transcends time and space. He is ineffable, sublime, transcendent, holy. He is totally other, the great I AM. Yet this same God sets aside the rights and privileges of his divinity and becomes a human being, and not just a human being but an embryo. He is born in a stable and laid in a feeding trough. He wears diapers, learns how to walk and talk, grows up as an ordinary man, learns a trade, and studies the Torah, though all the while he is God, too. After living on earth for a mere thirty years, he suffers and dies.

God born as a baby? God suffering humiliation? God dying on a cross? God buried in a tomb? How could this be? How could divinity be hidden in humanity? How could the one who lives outside time die at the age of thirty, the one who lives outside space live his whole life in Palestine? How could the one who controls history play a role within history that would profoundly affect its outcome? It is as if the author wrote himself in as one of the characters of the novel without making that character privy to the author's intent.

Gregory of Nyssa, one of the great thinkers and leaders of early Christianity, never outgrew his sense of wonder at the Incarnation. He said that if we want to see God at the pinnacle of his greatness, we must ponder what he called God's "condescension," that is, God's becoming a real human being in the person of Jesus Christ.

> It is not the vastness of the heavens and the bright shining of the constellations, the order of the universe, and the unbroken administration over all existence, that so manifestly displays the transcendent power of God as his condescension to the weakness of our human nature, in the way sublimity is seen in lowliness.[18]

Perhaps God's condescension provides a model for how we should pray. As God became lowly, weak, and vulnerable in Jesus, so we demonstrate those same qualities in prayer. Prayer calls on God to accomplish some good and godly purpose. Yet prayer also requires us to be humble, recognizing our neediness and helplessness. If anything, prayer is an act of submission to God. When we pray, we are like animals that roll over on their backs, exposing their underside. We are like Jesus hanging naked on the cross. We may be warriors, but warriors who have no weapon to fight with but prayer itself.

Truth in Tension

"The truth is always in the tension," I tell my students. It is in the tension between God as divine and God as human, between God's hidden will and God's revealed will, between God's plan for history and the prayers we say that shape the history God has planned.

No Christian writer explored this tension with greater insight and passion than Karl Barth. Early in his career as a pastor and theologian he rediscovered the transcendence of God and the power of prayer. In his mind the two were not mutually exclusive. If anything, he considered it incredible that an all-powerful and all-knowing God, the ruler of history, would command us to pray. In Barth's mind that command had authority. Why, he wondered, do we hesitate to pray "when it is the all-knowing and all-wise God Himself who commands us to come to Him with our requests?"

Still, a question remains. Considering how great God is, will our puny prayers make a difference? Barth believed that we must learn to live in a tension. It is true that God rules history by his "majestic counsel." Nevertheless, he invites us to pray, assuring us that our prayers make a real, eternal difference. He hears our requests in eternity, weighs them according to his plan, and answers them in time. So we must pray! As he put it, "There is a necessity of asking."[19]

It is in that tension that we find the motivation for prayer. We pray because we know that God is in complete control; he is moving history forward so that, in the end, his divine plan will be perfectly accomplished. But we also pray because God will use our prayers to accomplish that plan. God is the writer, the grand and glorious storyteller; we are the characters. We are real characters, too, not mere fabrications of God's imagination. The role we play contributes to the unfolding of the plot; the prayers we say influence the mind of the author.

This is how God has set things up. This is why he commands us to pray. It is the wonderful burden we must bear. In a flourish of brilliance, P. T. Forsyth concludes:

> Asking is a polar cooperation.... We do not ask as beggars but as children. Petition is not mere receptivity, nor is it mere pressure; it is filial reciprocity. Love loves to be told what it knows already. Every lover knows that. It wants to be asked for what it longs to give.[20]

LISTENING TO GOD

How, then, should we pray according to God's will? In my mind it requires a kind of rhythm. We should listen thoughtfully and carefully to God, and then we can ask wisely and boldly.

Listening should always come first. If we err, it should be on the side of listening. Better to say little to God, but say it well, than to say much but really say nothing at all. We will not pray rightly if we do not listen carefully. As spiritual writer Hans Urs von Balthasar says, "All of a sudden we just know; prayer is a conversation in which God's word has the initiative and we, for the moment, can be nothing more than listeners."[21] Søren Kierkegaard put it as well as anyone: "The true relation in prayer is not when God hears what is prayed for, but when the person praying continues to pray until he is the one who hears, who hears what God is asking for."[22]

We listen best when we meditate on Scripture, especially on the Psalms and on the prayers of the New Testament. Once we have listened, we can then make our requests—boldly, clearly, unapologetically, for we will be praying to God what he has already spoken to us. We will be praying Scripture, his very word, back to him. We may not know what will happen, but we can be sure something will happen. God will hear our prayers and answer them.

Perhaps that is why we should use the one formula for prayer that the Bible gives us. There are many prayers recorded in Scripture—the prayers of Moses, Nehemiah, Hannah, Deborah, Esther, Mary, Paul, even Jabez. But Jesus himself commands us to pray only one, the Lord's Prayer. It is startlingly simple.

First, it tells us to put first things first. We are praying *to God*, who is infinitely superior to ourselves. We should therefore show reverence and respect. Amazingly, we can call this holy God our Father. "Our Father in heaven, hallowed be your name."

Second, it calls for the establishment of *God's kingdom* on earth, not our own, and it is a kingdom of justice, peace, and love, not a kingdom of personal gain and power. "Your kingdom come, your will be done, on earth as it is in heaven."

Third, it asks God to meet our basic needs, both material and spiritual, all the while keeping in mind the needs of the larger community. We pray not just for our own individual needs but also for the needs of God's people around the world. "Give *us* today our daily bread. And forgive *us* our debts, as we also have forgiven our debtors."

Fourth, it invites us to acknowledge our vulnerability and weakness. We should never pray as if we were God's equal. When we pray, we approach God as finite and fallible human beings who need protection and deliverance. "And lead us not into temptation, but deliver us from the evil one."

Finally, it reminds us that God is in control, no matter how dreary and depressing life can be. "For yours is the kingdom and the power and the glory forever. Amen." This prayer sums up the will of God as we should pray it; it provides the template we should use.

My mind wanders back to my study of World War II. Someday a graduate student is going to study America's war on terrorism just as I studied the Second World War. She will page through the *New York Times* and *Newsweek,* experiencing the war on terrorism as if she were a contemporary and eyewitness, though of course she will already know how things turned out. She will feel the same kind of horror and helplessness about the September 11 terrorist attacks that I felt about Pearl Harbor, the atomic bomb, and the Holocaust. She will wonder why airport security wasn't more vigilant, why government officials didn't track down leads, why Americans were so dangerously complacent. She will read about individual acts of heroism and the tragic deaths of so many.

She will want to change what happened because she won't want to let some three thousand victims die. But she will be powerless to do a thing. It will already be in the past to her, just like World War II was to me.

But what will be the past to her when she studies the war is the present and future to us now. There is so much we don't know about the future, so much we can't control. It is pure mystery. History will unfold in ways that we cannot imagine and predict. The future will surprise us.

Some of these surprises could be wonderful. Scientists might discover the cure for AIDS. The President of the United States might reach a diplomatic breakthrough in the Middle East. NASA might begin a colony on Mars. Others could be as horrifying as Pearl Harbor, the atomic blasts that leveled Hiroshima and Nagasaki, and the Holocaust.

Nevertheless, though we don't know the future, we can pray to influence it. And when we pray, we won't have to speculate about what God might do or guess what God will do because we can claim what God has already promised to do, as it is recorded in Scripture. The hidden will of God is God's business. The revealed will of God is ours. That is the will we can and should pray, however mysterious prayer is.

If we dare.

QUESTIONS FOR DISCUSSION

1. How is it possible to influence the future through prayer? How does that work?

2. Think of a time or two when you were confused about the will of God while you were praying. What did you do?

3. What is the difference between God's revealed will and God's hidden will? What do you think of this distinction, especially as it applies to suffering?

4. How can you listen to God? Why is it so difficult?

5. What kind of guidance does the Lord's Prayer provide for us? Conclude by praying the Lord's Prayer.

CHAPTER 8

PRAYER IS NOT
ABOUT US!

The grass resolves to grow again,
receiving the rain to that end,
but my disordered soul thirsts
after something it cannot name.
JANE KENYON, "AUGUST RAIN, AFTER HAYING"[1]

It is not a perfect prayer if one is conscious
of oneself or understands one's prayer.
ST. ANTONY OF THE DESERT (251–356)

ANN HAD A FEELING THAT HER INFANT SON MICHAEL LOOKED different, though she couldn't put her finger on what it was. The doctors assured her that nothing was wrong. "Your baby is perfectly normal," they said. But her uneasiness persisted; her intuition would not rest. So doctors put him through a battery of tests.

Three weeks later the doctors reported the bad news. Michael had a rare disorder, Cri Du Chat Syndrome, which meant that Michael would suffer from poor muscle tone, lack of small motor control, mental retardation, and developmental delay for the rest of his life. So Ann and her family had to face the challenge of raising a

139

disabled child and integrating him into their home. It would be no easy task.

Ann's husband Rob recalls an incident that occurred about a year after Michael was born. A family in the church of which Rob was pastor asked him to call the elders of the church together to anoint their daughter with oil and to pray for her healing. Their daughter had cancer.

The request struck a raw nerve in Rob. It seemed almost ludicrous to him to pray for such a thing. He had been praying for Michael's healing for a year, with no apparent success. "Please God, replace the flawed gene," he had prayed time and again. "Make Michael whole and normal. I want to be grandfather to Michael's children. I don't want a wheelchair in my house!"

But duty is duty. He was this family's pastor. So he called the elders together and joined them in praying for the little girl's healing. Ironically, their prayers were answered, and the little girl was healed. This only added to Rob's frustration and pain. If God could heal her, why not Michael?

While Rob fought with God, refusing to accept the diagnosis as God's will, Ann surrendered and tried to make the best of it. She changed Michael's diaper, fed him, rocked him, talked and sang to him, stroked his hair, looked into his eyes, and smiled at him. Her mother's heart embraced him as a child who needed love. Her prayers for Michael were practical and immediate: "God, help Michael to eat better." "Make him responsive to my love." She rejoiced in the little victories. She considered it a major answer to prayer when, after months of almost complete indifference, Michael laughed aloud.

Their story took a strange turn when Michael was four years old. Michael had not yet learned to walk, even with the assistance of a walker. One day he crawled over to his walker, hoisted himself up, and started to walk across the kitchen floor toward the basement door. Not thinking that Michael was even close to becoming mobile,

Ann had momentarily left him alone in the kitchen. So she was not there to prevent him from falling down the basement stairs.

He landed on his head. Hearing a thud and the clatter of the walker, Ann dashed down the basement stairs after him. At first Michael wailed uncontrollably, and his entire body shook and twitched. Then he became completely still and silent, and he started to drift into a strange kind of sleep. His eyes rolled to the back of his head, his body became floppy, and his head swelled. It looked like he was dying.

Ann called Rob at the office, and he rushed home. They immediately drove Michael to the hospital. Neither said a word during the drive. Instead, they prayed quietly and with open hands, as if to say, "Whatever you will, we accept." They laid hands on him and prayed for his healing, just as they had done years earlier.

When they arrived at the hospital, the medical staff rushed him into the emergency room and ran him through a battery of tests. A very surprised doctor met with Rob and Ann some time later. "Something is peculiar here. There is absolutely no sign of injury, not even to his head. It's as if nothing happened. Your son is just fine."

As Rob said later on, "God chose to break in. He altered the course of what should have happened. The fall did no permanent damage, though at first it appeared that it did."

Rob and Ann have often wondered, as I wonder now: Why a healing the second time but not the first time? Is there a rational explanation? Did they have more faith the second time around? Had they become more worthy? Did they say the right words? Had God become more compassionate and merciful? They would answer "no" on all counts. But they would not stop there.

They would say that something extraordinary happened to them *because* Michael was not healed the first time around. For one thing, it increased their longing to know and follow God. For another, it changed the way they pray. They still pray for healings—their prayers for Michael after his accidental tumble down the basement stairs are evidence of that. But they pray now with *open hands,* a posture that symbolizes their desire to surrender their wills to God.

Rob puts it so well, "I used to use scripts when I prayed, telling God what my life should look like and what God should do to make it that way. But not any more." He pauses, smiles wryly, and then adds, "Prayer is dangerous. It will never leave us the same. We try to change our circumstances when we pray. But God uses our circumstances to change us. All prayer is a willingness to surrender the self to God." As Barbara Brown Taylor writes, "But there is more to prayer than the answer to prayer. There is also the pray-er, who is shaped by the praying."[2]

ASK GOD FOR WHAT YOU WANT?

Rob and Ann's story makes me wonder about the appropriateness of many of my prayer requests. I ask God for many things when I pray. And there's nothing wrong with that. Jesus even tells me to: "Ask and it will be given to you," he said. But what exactly *should* I ask for?

In 1540 Ignatius of Loyola founded the Society of Jesus, commonly known as the Jesuits, to advance the interests of the Catholic Church in Europe, which was at that time being challenged by the Protestants. But the Jesuits reached well beyond the borders of Europe. They became passionate about missions, too. By the end of the sixteenth century Jesuits had fanned out literally around the world to places as far away as China, India, Japan, and South America. To prepare recruits for the sacrifices and sufferings that surely awaited them, Ignatius wrote a manual for Christian growth entitled *The Spiritual Exercises.* He wanted to provide a practical and flexible tool the Jesuits could use as they traveled to and served in remote and dangerous places. Many of them died for their faith.

Ignatius also wanted to teach Jesuit missionaries how to pray. So *The Spiritual Exercises* provides guidelines for prayer. One guideline stands out as particularly unusual. It caught my attention the very first time I read it: "Ask God our Lord for what [you] want and desire."[3] It seems like an audacious prayer. Why not ask God for anything—a car, a yacht, a cabin, a castle, an empire to rule? It seems to appeal to base greed, beckoning God to do our bidding and indulge our appetite for whatever it is we crave, like an advertisement that appeals to our desire for wealth, beauty, and fame.

But Ignatius meant something very different. First, he tells us to *ask God* for what we want. That implies that the things we want most are beyond our reach, so we must ask God for them, as if we were children who cannot reach the goodies stored high on the shelf without Mom's help. Second, he tells us to ask God for *what we want,* which encourages us to ponder what we really do want in life. What longings run deepest in us, what desires do we have that only God can fill? What do we really want? What *should* we want?

I think about what I really want. Will my conscience allow me to pray for that?

Perhaps the reason why I don't pray more frequently and fervently is because I want the wrong things, lesser things, idols. When I do pray, it is usually for earthly things, like good health or job security. Not surprisingly, I don't pray with passion until I stand to lose those things. I don't pray for health until I'm sick; I don't pray for help until I'm in trouble; I don't pray for guidance until I'm confused about the future. I don't pray until something unwanted and unexpected disrupts my life and drives me to a point of desperation.

> *Perhaps the reason why I don't pray more frequently and fervently is because I want the wrong things, lesser things, idols.*

When life seems good to me, I don't pray as much. Why should I? I thank God for his blessings, to be sure, which is a worthy form of prayer that we often fail to practice when life is good, thus demonstrating an acute disregard for God's generosity. I ask God to continue showering me with those blessings. But my prayers often lack intensity until something bad happens. Then, like Peter when he slipped beneath the waves, I yell, "O Lord, save me!"

I remember an incident from many years ago that forced me to pray with passion. It was early evening. Lynda had just sent the neighborhood kids home and was drawing water for the first bath of the night. She asked me to call for Diana Jane, who was only three at the time.

"Diana Jane," I hollered. There was no answer, which was not unusual because Diana Jane liked to hide from us.

"Diana Jane," I called again with more authority. Still no answer.

I searched the house from top to bottom and looked outside. Then I ransacked the house again while Lynda called a few neighbors. Diana Jane was nowhere to be found. By this time I started to feel a slight wave of panic, like the first hint of nausea. I had to force myself to hold it at bay, concentrate on maintaining composure, and think about where she could have gone.

Friends came over and organized search parties. They checked the house once again, looking everywhere; they scoured the neighborhood, peeking into all the places where the kids liked to play; they made phone calls. No one could find her. After forty-five minutes of continuous searching I was beside myself with fear, as if spinning out of control in a free fall of terror. I imagined the worst—little Diana Jane had been abducted.

Finally we called the police. The officer knew that we were in a state of complete panic. He was very calm and kind. He said that it was standard procedure to search the house one more time, though he realized that we had already done it several times. He found her fast asleep under a bed, curled up in a bedspread right next to the wall. She was hidden so well that even he almost missed her. He picked her up and carried her outside.

I will never forget that moment. Even now my eyes fill with tears. I looked into Diana Jane's eyes, and she smiled at me as if to say, "What's all the fuss about?" I handed her to Lynda, and then I fell down on the ground and wept with relief.

I don't think I have ever prayed with greater passion and panic than I did when I thought that Diana Jane was lost. I was frantic to find her. I prayed fervently "for what I wanted" because I loved her dearly. When the incident was past, I returned to business as usual and prayed once again with the casualness of an elderly couple enjoying a Sunday afternoon drive, as if the only problem in the entire world—namely, my own—had just been solved.

It makes me wonder if our lack of zeal for prayer is the result of wanting things that are too confined to our own immediate concerns and earthly interests. As long as life runs along smoothly, we don't feel much need to pray. We pray—I mean, *really* pray—only when what we define as the norm (namely, our own happiness) is jeopardized, just like a person who will go to war only when the enemy is about to attack his own home. Thus, when cancer strikes, a spouse walks out, the stock market takes a nose dive, or a daughter marries a bum, then we pray.

Not that this is bad. I was perfectly justified when I prayed for Diana Jane. I had every reason to be as frightened as I was and to pray as fervently as I did. The problem is not that I pray for my own individual concerns. It is that I *limit* my prayers to that, which exposes my inclination to pray selfishly.

PRAYING ACCORDING TO CULTURE

I am slowly discovering that culture affects how I pray more than I would like to admit. Like most people, I want to be happy, successful, and prosperous. I want the same for my children and friends. In my weaker moments—and there have been many of them—I have prayed according to Western cultural privilege, not according to God's will. I have prayed for professional success, excellent health, safe vacations, and a happy home. I once prayed that God would motivate my son to study more diligently so that he would graduate from high school with a 4.0 average. I once prayed that my daughter would get a lead role in a play.

I am struck by how selfish my prayers have been—and still are. Perhaps I pray this way because the culture in which I live has awakened these desires in me and has promised to fulfill them, with God's help of course. Have my—have *our*—prayers become too selfish and worldly?

History itself appears to witness against us. The great spiritual writers seem to have viewed prayer differently than we do today. How so?

First, life for most people over the last two thousand years has been much harder than it is for us today. Before the discovery of anesthesia, penicillin, and other wonder drugs, many people never reached adulthood, dying at birth or from some childhood disease. Those who did reach adulthood had to work long and hard just to survive. Women had babies, sewed clothes, tended the garden, canned fruit, cleaned house, and cooked three square meals a day; men worked the fields or wielded a hammer in the blacksmith shop or tanned hides. Success, prosperity, and happiness were lofty goals, mostly beyond the reach of ordinary people. Not until fairly recently has technology, medical advances, and economic prosperity made it possible for so many people to enjoy the good life, at least in the West.

Our prosperity affects us in more ways than we can imagine. We don't—and probably can't—notice it until we step out of our circumstances and leave our comfort zone behind. It is like having pale skin at the end of a Midwestern winter. We don't notice how pasty white our skin looks until we spend a day on the beach in southern California. Sometimes we have to visit another culture to see how prosperous our society is and how selfish we have become, even when we pray.

Last summer I studied the "desert saints," an admittedly strange movement that flourished in the fourth and fifth centuries, just after Christianity had been established as the official religion of the Roman Empire. Many Christians were concerned that the church, after having suffered persecution for three centuries, had become too powerful and popular. Though church attendance skyrocketed, the standards of discipleship plummeted. A handful of dedicated Christians did not like what they saw and withdrew into the desert to counteract the worldliness of the church.

These desert saints ate a spartan diet, fasted and prayed, cultivated devotion to God, and served the needy. One man, John Cassian, was so fascinated by the movement that he traveled to the desert and lived among the desert saints for three years. He was especially impressed by their prayers. Observing how they prayed, he commented: "[Their prayer] contains no request for riches, no thought of honors, no petition for power, no mention of physical health or length of life. The author of eternity would have us ask nothing ephemeral, nothing paltry, nothing transient."[4] As Cassian said, we should pray for deliverance from our selfish interests, not for their fulfillment.

Second, many Christians around the world have suffered for their faith. It is hard for us living in the West to comprehend the magnitude of the persecution. The numbers are staggering. It is estimated that over seventy million Christians have died for their faith over the past two thousand years; forty-five million in the twentieth century! The Voice of the Martyrs reports that nearly two hundred thousand believers were martyred in the year 2000 alone.

Still, these numbers do not tell the real story. They are statistics about people we don't know and haven't heard of. These people had aspirations to live a long life, just as we do; who were loved by friends and family, just as we are; who hoped to conduct their affairs peacefully and quietly, just as we hope to. None of us can comprehend the enormity of those seventy million deaths.

Still, we can use our imagination. I am a historian by training and profession. I challenge my students to use their imagination when they study the history of the church, to get inside the experience of God's people as best they can, and to sympathize with the suffering of Christians who have had to pay the ultimate price for their beliefs. I tell the story of Perpetua, just twenty-two years old and a nursing mother, who died as a martyr in North Africa in the early third century. I recount the martyrdoms of Francis Ridley and Hugh Latimer, who encouraged each other to remain true to God as they were being burned at the stake under Mary's reign of terror in the sixteenth century. I remind them of the four hundred thousand Christians who were put to death under Idi Amin in Uganda in the early 1970s.

These martyrs prayed for deliverance. On some occasions their prayers were answered; on most occasions they weren't. In either case, they prayed for something else that was even more important to them than deliverance. They prayed that God would make them strong and faithful when they faced torture and execution, that their death would bring glory to God, and that the impact of their martyrdom would draw others to Christ.

Third, for some reason Christians in earlier times seemed to trust in the sovereignty of God more than we do today. They had a less grandiose view of what this world can offer and a more hopeful view of what life in heaven will be. While they did not disparage life on earth—after all, they did marry and raise children, work, and play—they believed that it was, even at its best, a mere hint of heaven, like an appetizer at the beginning of a sumptuous meal. However disappointing their life on earth, they trusted that God was preparing them for heaven. They kept their eyes on God's larger purpose, for they recognized that God was still God, even though their immediate circumstances seemed to indicate otherwise.

If they prayed for deliverance and God did not answer, they continued to pray, trusting that God was operating according to his own plan and timetable, not theirs. Unanswered prayer did not engender the kind of crisis that it often does for us today. Henri Nouwen, a spiritual writer who died recently, echoed the same theme:

Praying means giving up a false security, no longer looking for arguments which will protect you if you get pushed into a corner, no longer setting your hope on a couple of lighter moments which your life might still offer. To pray means to stop expecting from God the small mindedness which you discover in yourself.[5]

THE PROBLEM OF PROSPERITY

There is little we can do to change our cultural circumstances. That I was born into America's middle class was hardly my doing. It is a given, like the gene pool that determined my appearance and abilities. Besides, I like the circumstances of my life, at least for the most part.

Take this morning, for example. I rose early and took a run in a safe neighborhood. Then I prayed for awhile, sitting in my porch swing, surrounded by a beautiful lawn and blooming flowers. I ate a big breakfast and drove my youngest son, John, to basketball camp. Now I am sitting in a comfortable chair pecking away on my laptop. This afternoon I'm going to apply a first coat of varnish to French doors that divide the kitchen from the family room. Then, after attending John's late afternoon basketball game, I'll visit a local frozen yogurt parlor with a few friends and conclude the day by watching the Seattle Mariners play the Oakland Athletics in a crucial four-game series.

None of these activities is wrong or immoral. I never lied or cheated or stole to get what I now enjoy. I have no reason to feel guilty. The prosperity I experience is part of the air I breathe, the landscape in which I live. It is as familiar and normal to me as water coming out of the tap or as plentiful as food at the supermarket. But I forget how unusual it really is, considering the way most people around the world live. I wonder how it affects my prayers. I think it makes me too comfortable and self-satisfied, which is why I tend to pray only when prosperity is somehow threatened. I pray to keep life normal.

An entire movement has emerged in the last twenty-five years, called the "prosperity gospel," that justifies this approach to prayer. According to this movement, God wants us to claim the earthly inheritance that is ours by right. If we "name it and claim it," then we will get it. Health and wealth are ours for the asking; so is success in ministry, blissful marriage, perfect children, and happiness in life. It is all part of God's wonderful plan. One popular speaker some years ago put it blatantly this way: "Since I am the child of the King, I figure I deserve to live like a king"!

This is consumerism gone to roost in the church, a marketing mentality shaping the spiritual life. It treats God as if he were a genie in a bottle whose reason for existence, it would seem, is to respond to our every need, want, and demand. Never mind the values of the kingdom, as expressed in the Sermon on the Mount! Never mind the suffering of the world! Never mind Jesus' chilling warning that if we want to be his disciples, we must deny ourselves, take up the cross, and follow him!

I'm getting preachy, I know. But if I'm standing in the pulpit, railing against Christians in the West, I'm also sitting in the pew, listening, cowering, and probably scowling. I'm only preaching to myself. I am at fault, too.

PAUL'S "PROSPERITY"!

The apostle Paul serves as a useful counterpoint. We know more about him than any other character in the New Testament, except of course Jesus. Paul provides intimate biographical detail in books like Galatians, 1 Thessalonians, and 2 Corinthians.

There is little evidence that Paul ever prayed for the good life. He spent time in prison, yet he didn't pray for his release. He faced constant persecution, but he never asked to be delivered from it. Paul's life was hard and grueling, full of trouble and affliction. He suffered because he prayed, not because he failed to pray! He prayed that God would make him like Jesus and use him to win the world for Christ.

One passage in particular illustrates the point. Paul was in prison. He was writing to a small group of Christians living in Philippi. They loved Paul and prayed for his deliverance, and Paul believed that God would answer their prayers. "I know," he wrote, "that through your prayers and God's provision of the Spirit of Jesus Christ what has happened to me will turn out for my deliverance." Yet it didn't seem to matter much to Paul because something else mattered more, and that was his desire to honor Christ. "I eagerly expect and hope that I will in no way be ashamed, but will have sufficient courage so that now as always Christ will be exalted in my body, whether by life or by death. For to me, to live is Christ and to die is gain."

He shows surprising ambivalence in the passage. He pauses to think about what he wants more — freedom so that he can continue his ministry or death so that he can be with the Lord. He finally decides that he prefers freedom, but only for *their* sake. "I desire to depart and be with Christ, which is better by far; but it is more necessary for you that I remain in the body. Convinced of this, I know that I will remain, and I will continue with all of you for your progress and joy in the faith."[6]

WE PRAY TO KNOW GOD

Again, I ask myself, "What should I pray for? What do I really want?" Here the Bible points us in a new direction. It challenges us to ask a different question. In fact, *what* we pray for is not even the most important question. It is *why* we pray. We pray because God is worthy of our prayers. As it turns out, praying is not primarily about us at all. It is all about God.

We pray because what we really want, above all else and in the deepest places of our being, is *to know God*. That is our heart's desire, whether or not we know it consciously or feel it deeply. God created us; God sustains us; God redeems us. Everything we are—our ability to move and think, our capacity to love, our inclination to pray—

depends on God. He is like the air we breathe, like the food that feeds us, like the water that keeps us alive. C. S. Lewis wrote, "God designed the human machine to run on Himself. He Himself is the fuel our spirits were designed to burn, or the food our spirits were designed to feed on. . . . God cannot give us happiness and peace apart from Himself, because it is not there. There is no such thing."[7]

We pray because what we really want, above all else and in the deepest places of our being, is to know God.

We try to satisfy our deepest longings with lesser things. But it is all in vain. God himself has given us those things to enjoy, but he never wants us to mistake them for what is ultimate and essential. Thus, as Lewis observed, God withholds the happiness and security we want so that we won't settle for anything less than God himself. When our relationship with God is foremost to us, all other loves, longings, and pleasures actually increase. Lewis writes:

> When I have learned to love God better than my earthly dearest, I shall love my earthly dearest better than I do now. In so far as I learn to love my earthly dearest at the expense of God and instead of God, I shall be moving towards that state in which I shall not love my earthly dearest at all. When first things are put first, second things are not suppressed but increased.[8]

We pray, then, not to get something but to know someone, like a lover who relishes a relationship for its own sake and not for what he can get from it, such as pleasure or security or popularity. After the accident I missed Lynda for many reasons. I was overwhelmed by my circumstances, and I was overcome by my longing for her. At first I wished she were still alive to help keep life going at home. I needed her, at least in part, to do chores—to fold laundry, to keep the house clean, to cook meals, to do paper work, and to drive the kids to their activities. But I have long since mastered those responsibilities. Our home runs now as smoothly as a high-performance engine. I can cook, clean, care for the kids, and manage the home. I don't really need her as I used to.

Yet the ache remains because I miss *her,* not for what she could do but for who she is. I don't miss a wife in the abstract; I miss the person I was married to. I still see her face, I still smile at her idiosyncrasies, I still remember our late-night conversations. I even miss the fights. I have come to learn that the real pain of widowhood is the loss of the relationship with the one person I had given my heart to. I would be overjoyed if she were living as a quadriplegic in our home. At least I would have her back.

Of course, marriage is a distant second to a relationship with God. Whether we know it or not, we long for the presence of God, who is our true home. That is really why we pray. That God answers our specific requests is wonderful, just like vacation time is to us, however much we enjoy our jobs. But it is all secondary. It is enough simply to know God because a relationship with him is what we desire most.

The Old Testament story of Job underscores this point. Job is a good and righteous man. He has a big, happy family, great wealth, and a sturdy faith. Even God seems to marvel at Job. But Satan challenges God to a contest. Satan thinks that Job is a good and godly man *because* God has been so good to him. Deprive Job of his prosperity, Satan says, and Job will turn against God.

So God lets Satan make life miserable for Job. Job loses all his children, his wealth, and finally his health. Three friends visit Job to comfort him and to offer him advice. Relying on conventional wisdom, all three try to persuade Job to repent of his sins, for in their minds Job is suffering because he has sinned against God. He is getting exactly what he deserves. Job refuses to accept this explanation, believing that there is more going on than meets the eye. He knows he is not perfect, but he also knows that there are far worse people than he is who have not suffered to the same degree. Job argues with his friends, he struggles to understand, he wrestles with God. But he does not forsake his faith, nor does he curse God.

Finally, God becomes immediately, overwhelmingly, and undeniably present in Job's life. The story does not tell us how. Job describes this ineffable experience in a series of rhetorical questions that God asks of Job. The questions underscore God's greatness and power. The questions also make Job cower, put him in his place, and make him feel as small and insignificant as a fleck of dust. When the experience is over, Job can think of nothing to say, except—amazing as this sounds—to offer an apology for his presumption and ignorance. He is simply overwhelmed just being in the presence of God. Thus, he says to God:

> *I know that you can do all things;*
> *no plan of yours can be thwarted. . . .*
> *Surely I spoke of things I did not understand,*
> *things too wonderful for me to know. . . .*
> *My ears had heard of you*
> *but now my eyes have seen you.*
> *Therefore I despise myself*
> *and repent in dust and ashes.*[9]

Job encountered the living God in some kind of mystical experience. That much we know. The encounter stretched language and logic to the limit. Words failed him. Job became utterly still and silent, struck dumb by the unspeakable presence of God. He had no more questions, he made no more demands, he claimed no more rights. He simply bowed and surrendered because he had finally received what he most needed and longed for—an encounter with the living God.

WE PRAY TO GLORIFY GOD

There's a second reason why we pray. We also pray to *glorify God* because we long to catch a clearer glimpse of God's greatness, power, and beauty. God created the universe to set it ablaze with his glory.

Everything that exists manifests something of God's nature, his vastness or beauty or complexity. Humans are the ultimate and final expression of God's glory, the ones who bear his image. Thus, when we write a novel, run a business well, serve at a soup kitchen, love a spouse deeply, rebuild an automobile engine, and pray to God—especially when we pray—we bring glory to him. We show just how beautiful and holy God is. God created all things—especially human beings—to glorify himself.

Jesus himself was motivated to accomplish his earthly mission by his desire to glorify his Father. In fact, he would achieve glory for himself to the degree that he brought glory to his Father. "Father, the hour has come. Glorify your Son, that your Son may glorify you. . . . I have brought you glory on earth by finishing the work you gave me to do. And now, Father, glorify me in your presence with the glory I had with you before the world began."[10]

Nearly every Christian who has written about prayer emphasizes this point, as if following a script. Which they are—the biblical script. The glory of God is central to them. In their minds it is *the* primary motive for prayer. We can pray simply to indulge ourselves, which is not even true prayer. Or we can pray to glorify God. Eugene Peterson puts the contrast most sharply. We have a choice between two options; we can be egoistic when we pray, or we can be God-centered. There can be no compromise. When we pray, "We decide to leave an ego-centered world and enter a *God-centered world.* . . . But it is not easy. We are used to anxieties, egos and problems; we are not used to *wonder, God* and *mystery.*"[11]

Still, there's something about the idea of praying to the glory of God that makes me uneasy. It gives the impression that God is an egoist, wanting to draw attention to himself in the same way a boy in junior high brags about his athletic abilities. Is God so insecure that he needs to be reminded of his greatness? Is God so arrogant that he wants to be told how wonderful he is? It seems so juvenile, so unworthy of God.

Perhaps it is not as strange and offensive as it seems. When I lived in Chicago, I developed a friendship with a member of our church who was a master woodworker. About once a week I would join Skip in his shop late at night, and the two of us would "make sawdust" together, as he liked to put it. I marveled at his skill. He was a perfectionist. Once he finished a piece, he would stand back and gaze at it. "That is one beautiful piece of furniture," he would say with obvious satisfaction. Moved by its superior quality, he would momentarily forget that he had crafted the piece. He would admire his own creation as a thing that had value on its own. Still, I knew that every piece he finished was a reflection of the brilliance of this man. His own work glorified him.

God is the same way. After he had created the world, he said that it was good; after he had created humans, he said that they were very good. He took delight in what he had made. The beauty of creation reflects the brilliance of the Creator as a perfect piece of furniture reflects the brilliance of the craftsman. The wonder of redemption—Jesus' sacrificial work to save the world from sin, evil, and death—reflects even more brilliantly the glory of God.

THE "WHY?" AND THE "WHAT?"

Why we pray influences what we pray for. If we pray primarily to advance our own interests, then our prayers will become selfish and short-sighted, serving only ourselves. But if we pray to know God and to glorify God, then our prayers will put God right where he belongs, at the center of things. We will pray for those things that delight and honor God, even if we are praying for our own needs.

Thus, if we pray for healing, it will be to render better service to God. But if we continue to be sick, we will strive to honor God all the same, "whether in life or in death," as the apostle Paul put it. If we pray for a job, it will be to use our position and resources to build his kingdom and not our own. If we can't find a job, we will use our time and struggles to glorify God. We will put God first in everything.

Once we begin to pray to know God and to glorify him, then we can "pray for what we want," as Ignatius advised. In fact, *why* we pray and *what we pray for* are seamlessly connected. God is glorified when he answers our prayers, assuming we pray for the things that honor him—namely, our own transformation and the world's redemption (subjects we will explore in the next two chapters). God delights in our prayers, he listens with care, and he longs to answer them. God shows himself to be God when he does answer our prayers, but not if those answers reinforce the bad habits that need to be changed in us, like our selfishness and egoism.

I think about Rob and Ann's prayers for Michael. They pray now "with open hands," as they put it. That gesture is symbolic of what prayer means to them. It places God at the center, with Rob and Ann at his disposal. They still ask for "what they want," but always in a spirit of surrender. Of course they want Michael healed, and they probably always will. But they want something else even more. They want to know God; they want their lives to glorify God. As Rob said, they no longer follow a script. All prayer is surrendering to God because God is supremely wonderful and glorious and good. We were made for him, and we belong to him. All prayer, therefore, should lead to him.

QUESTIONS FOR DISCUSSION

1. What does it means to pray with "open hands"?

2. Why "pray for what you want," as Ignatius put it? What is the risk of praying such a prayer?

3. Think of some examples of "praying according to culture." Do you see this as a problem? Why?

4. Why is a relationship with God our deepest longing and need?

5. What does it mean to have God's glory in mind?

6. How would praying to know God and to glorify God change the way you pray?

CHAPTER 9

Prayer
Changes Us

True prayer is a lonely business.
Samuel Chadwick

Prayer is the most intimate activity I can share with
God, the utmost in self-revelation, the place where I can
bare my heart and soul before Him. In prayer I am
made vulnerable to God, my truest self is revealed, and
I find the promise that God is transforming this
ragamuffin into royalty—a son of the King.
Terry Glaspey

Hell.

It is a forbidden topic of conversation, except in very conservative religious circles. We squirm when it comes up, and we try to change the subject. We avoid churches that talk about it, and we skim over passages in the Bible that mention it. It is about as taboo a subject as incest.

Still, I am curious about hell. Like most people, I have heard all the conventional descriptions—steaming sulfur, raging fire, horrible screams, little red devils that wield pitch forks and taunt the damned. But that is not my interest here. I am more curious about how people land there. I used to think that God sends people there. I haven't changed my mind on that either, but I also think people choose to go there because they would find heaven an intolerable place to be. If heaven is the place where God is, they wouldn't want to have anything to do with it.

C. S. Lewis put me on to this idea. In his novel *The Great Divorce,* he tells the story of a group of people living in hell who take a bus tour of heaven. As they discover, at any point along the way they can choose to leave the tour group and stay in heaven. They are thus given a second chance. It is an extraordinary opportunity. Surprisingly, most of the tourists despise heaven and want to flee back to hell. It is too bright in heaven, too colorful, too solid, and too pure for them. It is so real that it hurts, like sunlight stinging the eyes after one leaves a dark movie theater. What makes heaven horrible to them is that God is there. They want to return to the shadows, as far away from God as possible.

Lewis shows in the novel that the primary difference between hell and heaven is not the temperature or smell or noise or pain. The real difference has to do with who is at the center. God is at the center of heaven. People who go to heaven, therefore, must be willing to live forever in the presence of someone who is infinitely superior to them and who will force them, by the sheer power of his presence, to conform to his greatness. Upon entering heaven, people will have to change. It is impossible *not* to change when living in the presence of God.

The self is at the center of hell. People in hell can live as egoistically and selfishly as they want, totally absorbed by themselves. As strange as it might sound, they *want* to be in hell. Hell is the only place where people can play God without any obstacles or competition. As a character in *The Great Divorce* says, "There are only two kinds of people in the end: those who say to God, 'Thy will be done,' and those to whom God says, '*Thy* will be done.' All that are in Hell, choose it."[1] Lewis actually borrowed this idea from Dante, who said that the door of hell is locked from the inside, not from the outside. Hell is where many people want to be.

WHAT DOES HELL HAVE
TO DO WITH PRAYER?

People who eventually land in hell insist that the world needs to change, *for their sake*. They want to be the center of things; they want the world to revolve around them. Hell gives them what they want, only the world they end up living in is as small as they are. People who go to heaven recognize that they need to change, *for God's sake*. They realize that God is at the center of things, and their responsibility is to conform to what he wants.

We pray because we want the world to be different, to be changed for the better, to be improved according to the will of God. So in our prayers we ask God to *change the world out there somewhere*, the world external to the self. Obviously "the world" that most concerns us is the world of our own immediate experience—home, church, neighborhood, local schools, city, and place of work. We pray that our spouse will become more loving, that our church will become more unified, that our community will become more open to outsiders.

But we forget that we need changing, too. We're not somehow above it all, with no faults of our own. We're not perfect, nor do we deserve to live in a perfect world. If every one of our prayers for the world "out there" were answered, we would probably be worse off than before, for we would remain as we are right now, egoistic and selfish, living in a world that had become much better than we are. We would only want to escape such a world. Hell would be a refuge for us.

So in our prayers we should also ask God *to change us*. He can then use us, as transformed people, to help change the world. We won't pray rightly, therefore, unless we're willing to admit that we need to change as much, if not more so, than the world that is external to ourselves.

If there is one experience that has exposed my faults and imperfections, it has been the experience of being a single father. Our home descended into virtual chaos after the accident. Catherine cried all the time; David became morose and angry; John whimpered and whined. The kids seemed to fight constantly, and they resisted my authority at every turn. As I look back now, eleven years after the accident, it seems almost comical to me, but only because the story has turned out well.

I kept a journal to record many of those early incidences and conversations to help me remember. One experience comes to mind; it is only one of many I could mention. Catherine was ten or eleven years old. It was bedtime. As usual, Catherine was dragging her feet, late to bed once again.

"Catherine, will you *please* get to bed."

"I have homework to finish."

"You should have done it earlier, as I asked. Now get to bed."

Ten minutes go by. Catherine is still in the living room, dawdling.

"Catherine, I want you in bed. NOW! No more excuses."

"I'm going to tell my teacher that you wouldn't let me get my homework done."

"Fine. Tell her, for all I care. You had time to do it. It's too late now. It's past your bedtime."

"I'm going to fail this assignment, and you don't even care."

"I've had it. Tomorrow night you must go to bed an hour earlier. You didn't do what I asked. You know the rules. I can't help it that you procrastinated."

"Now you're getting mad at me, too."

"I'm not mad. But I'm getting there. Do you want to have to go to bed an hour earlier for the next week?"

"O Daddy, you're so harsh with me. I want to love and trust you, but you make it so hard."

I was ready to explode. Then Catherine began to cry. I remember feeling so discouraged after such arguments that I would stay up until 2:00 A.M., fighting it out with God. I felt inadequate, helpless, and bewildered, not knowing how to respond to her disobedience and manipulation. Of course Catherine and I laugh about it now, but it wasn't so funny back then.

I prayed all the time. I asked God to change my children, and with good reason. They behaved like little monsters, and they seemed headed for disaster. Slowly but surely God answered my prayers. My children started to respond to discipline, do their chores, get along, and behave normally. Peace returned to our home. And I started going to bed earlier than 2:00 A.M.

But something else happened, too. I became less critical of my kids and more critical of myself. I already knew their weaknesses. They were too obvious to overlook. I prayed fervently that God would change them because they desperately needed changing. But I needed to change as well. I yelled and nagged too much, gave in too easily, and responded too emotionally to their fights and bad moods and irresponsibility. Catherine was actually right. I was too harsh.

I needed prayer as much as they did. Perhaps they behaved like "bad" children for that short stretch of time—fighting, whining, blaming, and defying. Then again, I behaved like a "bad" father, too—yelling, threatening, nagging, and lecturing. Ironically, God used their faults to correct my own. In the end God was gracious to us all. They became better children, and I became a better father.

Most homes are like mine, single parent or not. They seem to follow a similar pattern. Family members use the misbehavior of each other to excuse their own. A wife whines, "My husband is never home on time." Her husband responds, "She's such a crab when I'm home that it makes me want to stay away." A brother accuses a sister, "She comes into my room all the time without asking." She counters, "He's always taking my CDs. I can get them if I want to. They're mine." Accusations fly around like sparks from a fire that has just been stirred.

The problem is not confined to the home. I see it everywhere. Teammates blame each other for losing a big game. Politicians from both parties accuse each other of advocating policies that are bad for the country. World leaders point the finger at their enemies, charging them with responsibility for causing some international crisis. Everyone seems to be convinced that he or she is always right. This creates a problem. How can everyone be right and everyone else be wrong at the same time? It makes no logical sense.

> We need to ask God to take this fragile, selfish, flawed self of ours and make it more like him. God will answer that prayer.

Sometimes the results can be brutal, as in the case of marriages that end in a bitter divorce or international conflicts that lead to bloodshed and destruction. As long as no one is willing to change first, then nothing will ever change. Few people dare to look at themselves as critically as they view others. We demand that the world change according to our wishes. We even pray for it. Not surprisingly, we have made the world a hell on earth.

We need to pray for ourselves too, asking that God change us, whether or not he chooses to change the world around us. We need to ask God to take this fragile, selfish, flawed self of ours and make it more like him. God will answer that prayer. It is a prayer that makes his heart glad.

God's Greatest Gift to Us

Ultimately, God's greatest answer to prayer is something far different from what we could imagine. It is not what God does *for us* that demonstrates God's greatest answer to prayer; it is what God does *in us*. God wants to change us to his liking, not to change the world to our liking. As author and translator Eugene Peterson writes, "Prayers are not tools for doing or getting, but for being and becoming."[2]

Oswald Chambers believed that prayer changes us so that we can then help change the world. But it must begin with us.

To say that "prayer changes things" is not as close to the truth as saying, "Prayer changes me and then I change things." God has established things so that prayer, on the basis of redemption, changes the way a person looks at things. Prayer is not a matter of changing things externally, but one of working miracles in a person's inner nature.[3]

That is where God will begin—transforming our "inner nature." We can be sure of it because of who God is and what he has promised to do. Jesus used the example of an earthly parent to make the point. Most earthly parents, Jesus explained, are kind to their children. If children ask for something that seems reasonable, parents will give it because that is what good parents do. So if a son asks for a second helping of mashed potatoes, a mother is not going to give him moldy bread. If a daughter asks for a new pair of sweatpants, a father is not going to give her a gunny sack. It is of the very nature of parents to meet the needs of children, to respond favorably to their requests, to do what is best for them. That is what parents are supposed to do.

Then Jesus delivered the punch line. "If you then, though you are evil, know how to give good gifts to your children, how much more will your Father in heaven give the *Holy Spirit* to those who ask him."[4] God's greatest answer to prayer, his most precious gift, is not what we would naturally think. It is not things at all; it is himself, dwelling in our hearts.

Jesus' disciples must have been surprised by this punch line, perhaps even disappointed. I know I would have been. Putting myself in their place, I would have wanted something else. Instead of the "Holy Spirit," I would have hoped for "world peace" or "salvation for the lost" or "success in ministry" or "deliverance from evil" or "endless prosperity." Yet God's greatest gift, according to Jesus, is none other than the gift of the Holy Spirit, who takes up residence *inside us,* helping us to become more and more like the person God wants us to be, regardless of our circumstances.

God promises us himself. He pledges to send us the Holy Spirit to become present and active in our lives. John's gospel is relentlessly clear on this point. On the day before Jesus' trial and death, he spent one last evening with his disciples. They were filled with a sense of foreboding because they knew something was about to happen, though they weren't sure what it was. They wanted Jesus to remain with them, and they wanted things to remain as they were.

Jesus sensed their concern and addressed it. "But very truly I tell you, it is for your good that I am going away. Unless I go away, the Advocate [the Holy Spirit] will not come to you; but if I go, I will send him to you."[5] It would be the Spirit's job, Jesus said to his disciples, to empower them for ministry, to convict the world of sin, to remind them of Jesus' teachings, and to give them peace in the midst of tumult.

The Holy Spirit would not make life easy for them. But Jesus was convinced that the presence of the Spirit would serve their best interest because God as a Spirit would be working *inside them,* enabling them to follow him. The apostle Paul argued similarly when he told believers in Ephesus to keep on being "filled with the Holy Spirit" because the Spirit would transform them into extraordinary people, characterized by joy, peace, and love.[6]

OUR GIFT TO GOD

But do we really want the gift of the Holy Spirit? Do we dare ask for that gift in prayer? I wonder. The price might be greater than we imagine. I think I would rather play it safe and ask for something less threatening and more convenient, like success or wealth or power. Do I really want the Spirit of God working inside me to change my life?

The experience of the disciples of Jesus adds substance to my concern. Jesus told them to wait in Jerusalem until he sent the Holy Spirit. They waited for ten days, praying and fasting. What did they think about during those ten days? Could they have imagined what eventually happened to them in the years that followed?

After being filled with the Spirit, they fanned out across the Roman world, telling people about Jesus, healing the sick, and serving human needs wherever they found them. Overflowing with the Holy Spirit, they became effective witnesses and living examples of what God can do in the lives of ordinary people who belong to him. By the time they began to die off, they had started little churches throughout the Roman world and left such a huge impression on society that even emperors grumbled about their influence and targeted Christians for persecution. It all sounds so dramatic. Wouldn't it be exciting if we could be transformed as they were? If we could accomplish what they did? If we could experience the power of the Spirit in the same way?

I'm not so sure. What happened *in them* seems very compelling to me. What happened *to them* as a result fills me with terror. The disciples faced constant opposition, experienced deprivations of every kind, and died martyrs' deaths because they had been filled with the Holy Spirit. God transformed them, worked wonders in them, and influenced the world through them—all by the Spirit's power. But at what a price! Their success intrigues me; their suffering repels me. Could I have one without the other? I don't think so.

God did nothing less than make them like Jesus. He will do the same with us. That is the goal, if we dare to ask for it. It is both the prize and the price, all wrapped into one. As Paul says of the transformative work of the Holy Spirit, "Now the Lord is the Spirit, and where the Spirit of the Lord is, there is freedom. And we all, who with unveiled faces contemplate the Lord's glory, are being transformed into his likeness with ever-increasing glory, which comes from the Lord, who is the Spirit."[7]

Jean-Pierre de Caussade echoes this same theme. God's real business is to make us like living letters to the world that tell everyone what God wants to do with human life.

We are in an age of faith, the Holy Spirit no longer writes gospels, except in our hearts; saintly souls are the pages, suffering and action the ink. The Holy Spirit is writing a living gospel with the pen of action, which we will only be able to read on the day of glory when, fresh from the presses of life, it will be published.[8]

There is much good that we can accomplish on our own. We can learn to read and write, swing a golf club, balance a checkbook, clean a house, drive a car, raise children, discipline our appetites, even improve our character. But we cannot become like Jesus without God's Spirit working inside us any more than a surgeon can perform open heart surgery on herself. The most that we can do is to surrender ourselves to God or, as Paul writes, to offer ourselves to God as "living sacrifices." That means surrendering everything we are and everything we have—our bad habits as well as good ones, our silly idiosyncrasies, our darkest secrets, our amazing talents, our meager savings—all to God.

But we cannot become like Jesus without God's Spirit working inside us any more than a surgeon can perform open heart surgery on herself.

The holiness movement of the nineteenth century used the word "consecration" to make the same point. Leaders of the movement recognized how utterly weak and fickle human nature is. We have little power to change ourselves, for the very self we appeal to for the motivation and power to effect change is the very self that so desperately needs to be changed. So we must consecrate—that is, entrust—ourselves to God and ask him to do in us what we cannot do for ourselves. Hannah Whitall Smith communicated this idea in the most appropriate way possible—as a prayer.

I have tried keeping myself, and have failed, and failed, most grievously. I am absolutely helpless. So now will I trust thee. I give myself to thee. I keep back no reserves. Body, soul, and spirit, I present myself to thee as a piece of clay, to be fashioned into anything thy love and thy wisdom shall choose.[9]

The story of the prodigal son shows, through a subtle shift in language, the difference between a person who egoistically demands something from God and the person who humbly surrenders to God. As Harry Emerson Fosdick observed, early on in the story the son demanded something from his father. He asked for his inheritance, a heartless request considering ancient Near Eastern custom, which would not allow a son to take his inheritance until after his father died. He said, "*Give me* my share of the estate." Then, after his father complied, he fled his home and wandered into a far country, where he squandered his inheritance in vain and wasteful pursuits. Soon he became desperate and hired himself out to a pig farmer.

He finally came to himself, realizing that he would do better as a servant in his father's house than on his own. When he returned home, he did not repeat the same request that he had made earlier. Instead, he said to his father, "*Make me* like one of your hired servants." But his father welcomed him back into the home, not as a servant but as a son.

Note the change of prayer from "Give me" to "Make me." Fosdick concludes:

> Whether through experience of sin or sorrow or hard practical struggle we come to a real maturity, we always tend to grow out of crying to God "Give me" into the deeper prayer "Make me." In a word, we cease valuing God merely because of the things he may give, and we come into the love of God himself and the desire to be made over by him.[10]

This is the act of consecration. We offer ourselves to God, asking that the Spirit do with us what is best, though it may be what is hardest, too.

GOD'S TOOL OF TRANSFORMATION

God's greatest gift to us is the Holy Spirit; our gift to God is simply ourselves, offered as living sacrifices. Now only one thing remains. God needs a tool—say, a chisel—to do this transforming work. The tool God uses most often is adversity—that is, difficulty, hard times, irritations, struggles, opposition, and suffering.

Paul is especially clear on this point. Though most English translations use the word "suffering" in Romans 5, the Greek word can also be translated "adversity," "affliction," or "hard times." Paul argues that God uses adversity to transform us. "We also glory in our sufferings, because we know that suffering produces perseverance; perseverance, character; and character, hope. And hope does not put us to shame, because God's love has been poured into our hearts through the Holy Spirit, who has been given to us."[11] The book of James adds, "Consider it pure joy, my brothers and sisters, whenever you face trials of many kinds, because you know that the testing of your faith produces perseverance. Let perseverance finish its work so that you may be mature and complete, not lacking anything."[12]

Adversity is necessary for growth in the spiritual life. For example, take growth in patience. It is not my favorite virtue. I drive my car as if I'm a man on a mission. I'm easily irritated by people who drive slower than the speed limit and by traffic lights that turn red just before I reach the intersection. Exercising patience is about as natural to me as driving slowly. Not surprisingly, traffic jams, flat tires, road repairs, and other delays force me to practice patience, which I don't like but know I need. Similarly, conflicts among my children challenge me to become gentle, tumult in the home to find peace in God, exhaustion to rest in his grace.

Is there another way? I wish there was. But my understanding of human nature sobers me. I cannot fathom why there is so much suffering in the world. Why does God allow it? Much of it seems useless to me, or worse, destructive beyond measure. Some people don't overcome it, transcend it, or even survive it. Instead, they stumble and fall, never to rise again, through no fault of their own either. They simply crumble under the pressure. Sooner or later everyone does, for we all have our breaking point. So I refuse to romanticize suffering. If anything, I view suffering with horror, and I recoil from it. I have seen too many people fail to bounce back.

Yet I cannot fathom what we would do without suffering either. I have come to this conclusion with great hesitation. Adversity strips us down, exposes us, and breaks us, all prerequisites for genuine growth in the spiritual life. Sometimes old cars have to be torn apart before they can be properly restored to mint condition. Suffering makes us aware of our need, our weakness, and our sinfulness. It drives us to God.

In our adversity God becomes present and active. The gift he gives us in our hour of deepest need is himself, nothing more and nothing less. Rotting in prison?—God is there, leading us to repentance. Lying on our deathbed?—God is there, comforting us. Betrayed by a friend or lover?—God is there, caring for us. Squashed by the competition?—God is there, restoring hope in us. For some reason this is the only way we seem to learn, the only way we overcome our attachment to the world, the only way we die to our egoism and selfishness. We ask God for tangible gifts, many of them reasonable and worthy of prayer. But what we really need is simply God, present and active in our lives.

There is a cross etched on the wall of cell 21 in the basement of the Death Block in Auschwitz. A brave Polish resistance officer, Stefan Jasienski, used his fingernails to etch it during his imprisonment. It was a frantic plea, his soul's cry for deliverance. Why the cross in a Jewish prison camp? Why only in that cell?

Two cells away Father Maximilian Kolbe was being starved to death for something he never did. In 1941 a fellow prisoner escaped. To smoke out the escapee, a Nazi officer forced the prisoners from the block to stand at attention all day long in the summer heat, without food or water. When the escapee was not found, the officer announced that ten men would have to die in the place of the one who was missing. One of the ten men selected, Franciszek Gajowniczek, cried out in despair. "Oh, my poor wife and children will never see me again."

It was then that Father Kolbe stepped forward. He attempted to kiss the officer's hand. When asked what he wanted, he told the officer that he wanted to die in Gajowniczek's place. The officer agreed to his request. He sent him to the starvation cell of the Death Block. But Kolbe would not die. He survived for two weeks without food or water. The Nazis finally killed him with a lethal injection. While he remained alive, Kolbe led the other nine men in fervent hymns and prayers. The Death Block became, as a janitor later wrote, "like a church." Several years later Jasienski etched the cross in his cell as a memorial to the faith of these men. Gajowniczek, the man whose life was spared by Kolbe, survived the camp and saw his family again. He did not die until 1997.[13]

I have no reason to doubt that Kolbe would have become a good man, even if he had never been in prison. But he would not have become a heroic man. He needed the Death Block for that. Adversity allowed him to demonstrate unusual courage, to love sacrificially, even to die a martyr's death. His circumstances were extraordinary, to be sure. We may never have to endure what he did, God willing. But we will have to face some degree of adversity all the same, perhaps only on a more modest scale. Like Kolbe, the real heroes in life are those who respond to adversity with dignity, faith, and patience. All we must do is be attentive to the little irritations and problems we face every day, asking the question, "What is God trying to do in my life?" And then pray, "God, use this adversity to transform me."

HOW THEN SHOULD WE PRAY?

Strangely, though we realize how desperately we need to change, we stubbornly resist it, too. That stubbornness affects our faith. We want

God on our terms, to make life nice for us and to cut a safe and secure path for us, with no hassles, no inconvenience, and no suffering. Unfortunately, there is no such God, and there is no such life. As M. Scott Peck wrote,

> Life is difficult. This is a great truth, one of the greatest truths. It is a great truth because once we truly see this truth, we transcend it. Once we truly know that life is difficult—once we truly understand and accept it—then life is no longer difficult. Because once it is accepted, the fact that life is difficult no longer matters.[14]

Yet God can use difficulty to make us better people, if we are willing. Armand M. Nicholi Jr., a practicing psychiatrist and professor at Harvard University, had taught for years on the life and worldview of Sigmund Freud when a student enrolled in the class suggested that Nicholi include a counterpoint to Freud, someone who represented a clear alternative. Nicholi thought the student's suggestion was sound. He decided to use C. S. Lewis as that counterpoint.

The similarities between the two men startled Nicholi. Both men were precocious, lost important loved ones at a young age, related uncomfortably to their fathers, and while teenagers rejected their family's religious belief system. But Lewis returned to faith (in his case, Christianity) as an adult. The impact on the course of Lewis's life, Nicholi discovered, was dramatic.

It appears that Lewis's faith in God turned his life in a different direction, one that veered sharply from Freud's. While Freud had trouble maintaining intimate relationships, Lewis developed deep friendships that lasted a lifetime. While Freud struggled with jealousy, suspicion, and unhappiness most of his adult life, Lewis became healthy and joyful. While Freud's losses and suffering wore him down until he finally committed suicide, Lewis's losses appeared to ennoble him. In short, Lewis was transformed by his faith in God, becoming healthier and happier, even though, like Freud, he encountered difficulties, faced adversity, and experienced disappointments throughout his adult life.

Social scientists have only recently begun to study what makes people healthy and happy. Sincere faith in God and consistent religious practice appear to contribute to their mental, physical, and emotional well-being. For example, religious faith helps people bounce back more quickly from sickness and loss, deepens relationships, enriches marriage and family, and enhances overall well-being. There are many reasons for this. But surely one of them is that faith helps people to respond more positively to adversity, to adjust more successfully to difficulties, and to change when there is a genuine need for it. Faith seems to empower people to become stronger, healthier, and wiser.

Either we can view the world as a place that needs changing for our sake, or we can ask God to use the world to change us for his sake.

God is eager and willing to do whatever it takes to help us. But we must be willing to turn to him, face ourselves, and change. It all comes down to a choice. There will be no fanfare; few will take notice. Either we can view the world as a place that needs changing for our sake, or we can ask God to use the world to change us for his sake. Not that one is more important than the other. The world does need to change, but so do we.

Will God answer our prayer? Will he transform us? Most certainly he will, though we do not—and cannot—know how. God's Spirit must plunge deep into our lives. We don't know the tenth of what must be done and what God will do. We wouldn't want to know either, for it would overwhelm us. All we need to know is that God will do it. He will answer our prayers in ways that are incomprehensible to us now but will make perfect sense later on when we will see the results of God's extraordinary work in our lives.

O. Hallesby says it so well. "'But why doesn't He answer me?' you ask perplexed. He has answered your prayer. He has entered into your life, through the door which you in your helplessness have opened for Him. He is already dwelling in your heart. He is doing the good work within you."[15]

QUESTIONS FOR DISCUSSION

1. Recall a few instances when you wanted your circumstances to change or perhaps the people around you to change. Think of some reasons why it is so hard to change ourselves.

2. Why is the Holy Spirit God's greatest gift?

3. How can you begin to offer yourself to God as a living sacrifice?

4. Why is adversity so necessary in the Christian faith?

5. Reflect on the adversity you are facing. How might God use that adversity to change you?

CHAPTER 10

THE EPIC STORY

It is not that our prayers are not answered,
it is that we do not accept the answer.
KOSTI TOLONEN

ON WEDNESDAY, JULY 24, 2002, MARK POPERNACK, A MINER WORK-ing deep below ground, accidentally drilled into an adjacent aban-doned mine that had been flooded for some time. A wall of water rushed into the shaft where miners were working, sixty million gal-lons moving at sixty miles an hour. Unable to outrun it, the min-ers—nine of them—were inundated by the water. They all knew that it was a matter of minutes before they would drown. "The scary part was watching the water rise, knowing that you don't have a way out," said Dennis Hall, one of the nine. The water kept coming until it was over their heads.

Tying themselves together so that they would survive or perish as a group, they made their way to a small compartment, measuring only four feet high, which the water had not yet flooded. There they hud-dled, water lapping at their feet, trapped 240 feet below ground. It was pitch black, cold, wet. They smelled bad air. If the water didn't get them, they thought to themselves, toxic air or hypothermia would.

The first moment of hope came when rescue workers broke through the mine shaft with a small hole to pump in warm, fresh air. The miners tapped on the pipe nine times, indicating that all nine were still alive. Then they waited. As the hours passed, the men encircled the six inch hole to try to keep warm and to breathe the fresh air. They used one flashlight at a time, and then for only a few hours a day.

They also shared their thoughts with each other. "Anything imaginable—about your family, the last thing you said to your family before you left for work that day," Harry (Blaine) Mayhugh said. They wrote notes to their family to give parting words. Mayhugh explained that he wanted "to write my wife and kids, you know, to tell them that I love them." One wrote to his daughter, "I thought about you 'til the end." They did their best to encourage each other. "We had high points and low points," Mayhugh said. "When somebody'd get low, we'd all work to cheer them up. Then you'd be down, and everybody worked on you."

At one point, however, their hope almost died. For several hours they had heard the rumblings of a large drill bit that was opening a shaft big enough to haul them out. Suddenly the noise stopped. The silence continued for eighteen agonizing hours, long enough to make that dark, cold, wet mine feel like a tomb. The miners started to think that something had gone desperately wrong. Perhaps the rescue workers had given up, assuming that they were dead.

It was a very different scene above ground. Rescue workers were laboring around the clock, frantic to save the men. The drilling had stopped because the drill bit had broken and needed to be replaced, which required hours of precious time. Meanwhile, family and friends huddled in a nearby volunteer fire department—hoping, waiting, comforting each other. It seemed that everyone was praying. Signs appeared in virtually every window. "PRAY FOR THE MINERS." A candlelight vigil on Friday at All Saints Catholic Church drew three hundred people. Supporters erected an altar with nine figurines of the miners.

The mine is situated just ten miles from where United Flight 93 crashed on September 11, killing all forty aboard but saving the lives of countless others who were undoubtedly targeted by the terrorists. Family members of the passengers of that doomed flight sent a letter of support to the friends and family of the miners. People from surrounding communities sent food. The entire country was caught up in it. Millions prayed that the miners would be rescued.

People in the community and around the United States—to say nothing of the miners themselves!—were both stunned and relieved when, after long hours of waiting, the drilling resumed. The rescue workers eventually reached the men and pulled them to safety. Nearly everyone attributed their survival to the grace of God. It was an answer to prayer, they said. A friend and neighbor of one of the miners said, "The mines can be hell, but there are miracles that can happen, too." The owner of a nearby restaurant commented, "We went from feeling like somebody slapped us to knowing that our prayers are answered."

But it was a construction worker from the community who summed up the feeling of relief and gratitude best. "You think that that's just the way things go, and that tragedy is part of life. Something like this sure can change the way you look at things."[1]

AGAINST ALL ODDS

I try to put myself in the place of those miners. Those eighteen hours of silence must have been almost unbearable, like waiting for one's execution. The drilling had stopped; it seemed the rescue workers had quit. The miners felt utterly alone, forsaken, abandoned. It was only a matter of time before they would perish. Eighteen hours of agony and uncertainty and terror, 240 feet below ground, in a place that must have seemed like hell to them.

And all they could do was wait, hour after hour, for help to arrive, if there was ever going to be any help. Yet those nine men never stopped believing, however bad the odds were. They prepared themselves for the worst—death. But they hoped and prayed for the best—deliverance.

Eighteen hours is not a long period of time, unless of course you are trapped 240 feet below ground, expecting to die at any moment from drowning or hypothermia or asphyxiation. During such a traumatic experience time becomes relative. I'm sure it felt like eighteen days, or even longer.

This is true for all of us at some point in our lives. The lapse of time between promise and fulfillment, between prayers uttered and prayers answered can seem interminable, far too long to maintain hope and to persist in prayer. But sometimes that is exactly what we must do—keep hoping and praying, for eighteen hours or eighteen days or eighteen years, even when there doesn't seem to be one good reason to continue.

It is easier said than done. I have endured many periods in my adult life, especially since Lynda died, when I have waited, hoped, and prayed with hardly a breath of faith left in me, as if I were gasping to believe that God was still there for me.

One incident in particular comes to mind. About a year after the accident I received a packet of articles in the mail from a relative who wanted to prepare me for the worst but also help me set a course that would bring healing to my family. The articles spelled out the findings of social scientific research on the long-term impact on children of the loss of their mother. That evening I followed our usual bedtime routine, finished cleaning up the kitchen, put on a CD of Faure's *Requiem,* and then collapsed into my favorite rocking chair. I just sat there for a while, trying to summon the energy to do one of the ten things that still needed to be done.

Then I remembered the articles. I began to read them with a strange sense of foreboding, as if I was reading the future obituary of my children. I learned that the impact of early childhood loss of a mother is often devastating, especially after children reach adulthood. Children who lose mothers at a young age are inclined toward depression, have difficulty developing lasting attachments, and often flounder through life, moving from job to job and relationship to relationship.

I sat there stunned, and I felt myself sinking into despair. "It doesn't matter what I do or how much I pray. The odds are stacked against me. I can expect nothing but a lifetime of pain. The bleeding is never going to stop." In that moment I thought that my children were destined for a lifetime of suffering—poor school performance, friendlessness, divorce, chronic depression. It took everything in me to continue to believe that the tragedy would not have the final word, that our destiny as a family would not follow the bleak statistics I read about in those articles. I hit a low point that night, one that continued for some time. I braced myself for the worst to happen.

NOT IN THAT WAY

What if we have to wait for a long time—longer than the miners did, longer even than I did—to have our prayers answered and to see signs of God's redemptive work in our lives? One option, of course, is to assume that God isn't going to answer our prayers at all, so we should quit praying.

It could be that there is no such thing as unanswered prayer. What we interpret as "no" might really be "not in that way" or "not yet."

But there's another option. It could be that there is no such thing as unanswered prayer. What we interpret as "no" might really be "not in that way" or "not yet." In other words, the waiting itself might be necessary, creative, and useful, like watching a forest gradually recover from a devastating fire until it becomes more beautiful than before.

Unanswered prayer *according to our perspective* does not mean unanswered prayer according to God's. Likewise, unanswered prayer *in the present moment* does not mean unanswered prayer next month or next year or perhaps in the next century.

Sometimes we think too small, like an infant whose world is no bigger than its crib. We assume we know what is best for us, which influences how we pray and when we stop praying. But the landscape of life is much bigger than what our sight-line will allow us to see, especially in the case of prayer. When we pray, we must keep that larger landscape in mind, as if we were an explorer who knows that there is more to a mountain range than what the naked eye can see. What we think is good for us, considering our immediate circumstances, might not be good at all in the long run. It is all a matter of perspective.

Country and Western singer Garth Brooks, of all people, explores this idea in his song "Unanswered Prayers." In the song Brooks reflects on attending a high school football game years after he graduated. There he runs into his old high school sweetheart, whom he has not seen since graduation. He introduces his wife to her and then tries to make small talk. His mind wanders back to those many years before when he wanted to marry her more than anything and prayed each night that "God would make her mine." He remembers thinking that if God granted him that one wish, he would "never ask for anything again."

But meeting her twenty years later sobers him. She isn't "quite the angel" that she appeared to be. She has changed. They try to reminisce, but after a few minutes the conversation trails off. She finally leaves. Then he glances at his wife, a pure gift to him, and he realizes that God has answered his prayers in a way that far exceeded his longings and expectations.

> *Sometimes I thank God for unanswered prayers*
> *Remember when you're talkin' to the man upstairs*
> *That just because he may not answer doesn't mean he don't care*
> *Some of God's greatest gifts are unanswered prayers.*

As Søren Kierkegaard wrote, "This is our comfort, because God answers every prayer; for either he gives what we pray for, or something far better."[2]

John Calvin was quietly converted to the Christian faith sometime in the early 1530s. Already an educated scholar and published author, he planned to retire from public life and pursue his scholarly studies. While traveling to Strasbourg in 1536, Calvin was forced to take a detour through Geneva to avoid some minor war. One of the leaders of the Reformation in Geneva, Farel, heard that Calvin was staying at the local inn for a night. He visited Calvin and asked him to remain in Geneva to help organize the fledgling Reformation church that had only recently been started. Calvin refused because it was not in his plans. Farel put pressure on Calvin, insisting that he stay. Finally he threatened Calvin. If Calvin would not contribute to the work there, Farel declared, God would condemn him.

So Calvin stayed in Geneva, for the rest of his life as it turned out, except for a brief period of three years when a hostile city council forced him to leave. He spent twenty-five years there because of a chance encounter with Farel. The course his life took was not what Calvin had planned; it was not what he wanted; it was not what he prayed for. But it is what was given to him. Strangely, it was an answer to a prayer that he never prayed.

Calvin knew it, too, but only by looking back on the many years he spent in Geneva. As he wrote in his preface to *The Commentary on the Book of Psalms* about his first years of ministry:

> Being of a disposition somewhat unpolished and bashful, which led me always to love the shade and retirement, I then began to seek some secluded corner where I might be withdrawn from the public view; but so far from being able to accomplish the object of my desire, all my retreats were like public schools. In short, while my one great object was to live in seclusion without being known, God so led me about through different turnings and changes, that

he never permitted me to rest in any place, until, in spite of my natural disposition, he brought me forth to public notice.[3]

During his years in Geneva Calvin preached through almost the entire Bible; his sermon notes provided material for his commentaries. He became involved in Genevan politics and helped to write the city charter, started the silk worm industry, founded an academy, formed deep friendships with many Reformation leaders, and provided leadership for a movement during its formative stages. His influence continues to this day.

Where would the church be if Calvin had refused to serve as a pastor and leader of the church in Geneva? Yet Calvin did not aspire to it, plan on it, or desire it. It was not what he would have considered an answer to prayer. But I for one am glad and grateful that God answered his prayers in a way he did not expect or want. We are the richer and wiser for it.

Instead of unanswered prayer, perhaps there are only answers to prayer that we don't want, can't foresee, and wouldn't ask for. I am not arguing that we should never pray because our prayers might somehow be wrong, off the target, or misdirected. We can hardly avoid having expectations when we pray. After all, we do *ask* for things when we pray, and rightly so. We can and should pray for our heart's desire.

> *Instead of unanswered prayer, perhaps there are only answers to prayer that we don't want, can't foresee, and wouldn't ask for.*

What I am suggesting, however, is that we pray with *flexibility* as well as boldness, holding our expectations with a light touch and looking for signs that God is answering our prayers in a way that is different from what we wanted and asked for. Unanswered prayer from our limited perspective might in fact turn out to be answered prayer from a larger frame of reference. God may say "no" to our request because he wants to give us something different and in the long run better, though it might not seem that way at first.

O. Hallesby suggested that if there is any way God can surpass our requests, he will, though Hallesby acknowledged that such an answer to prayer might appear to us to be unanswered prayer. Using Luther as an example, Hallesby writes, "As Luther says, 'We pray for silver, but God often gives us gold instead.' Every time Jesus sees that there is a possibility of giving us more than we know how to ask, He does so. And in order to do so he often has to deal with us in ways which are past our finding out."[4]

NOT YET

I pray as if prayer were like a short story—a quick and easy read, with few pages, simple plot, and clear story-line. But God wants me to pray as if prayer were like an epic that unfolds on a huge landscape and over a long period of time. If salvation history teaches us one thing, it is that God's redemptive work requires a great deal of time and space. What God is up to extends far beyond what the eye can see and the mind can imagine. We cannot be in a hurry. God has his own sense of timing, which is usually slow when we think it should be fast and fast when we want it to be slow.

Take, for example, the coming of the Messiah. It is a lesson in divine timing. Why did God wait so long? Who knows? But when conditions were just right, Jesus was born in a small town and, after thirty years of living an ordinary life, launched a public ministry that lasted only three short years. During those three years Jesus kept up a furious pace. And that was only a warm-up to the warp speed of the last week of his life, when the destiny of the entire human race and the future of the world hung in the balance.

It seems that God had all the time in the world before Jesus came and then almost ran out of time once Jesus arrived. Salvation history loped along for centuries, like a tired horse that can hardly walk. Then suddenly it picked up speed, like a bullet shot from a gun. Countless people had prayed for centuries that the Messiah would come. Eventually their prayers were answered, though most of them were long gone. Precious few were privileged to see Jesus, know him, and follow him, and even then many failed to recognize who he was.

Or take the growth of the early church. Rome was near the zenith of its power when the church got its start. The city of Rome was dazzling, its court the envy of the world, its emperors rich and powerful and corrupt. If *People Magazine* and *Newsweek* had existed back then, they would have run cover story after cover story on the wealth and splendor of Rome and its people.

No one would have taken much notice of the Christian movement, which began in Palestine, the backwaters of the Roman world, and spread first among the lower classes and the powerless—slaves, women, and foreigners—as well as the more privileged. In comparison to Rome it was tiny and insignificant, hardly worth noticing. It took centuries for the movement to get on its feet. Yet this fledgling movement would eventually overtake the Roman world and encircle the globe. When Rome collapsed, the church was poised to fill the vacuum. What began as a tiny mustard seed grew into a great tree. Who could have foreseen such a thing?

When we are ready to quit, God might be just warming up. When we have decided to classify a prayer as unanswered, God might be just about to answer it.

It is hard to wait for answers, especially when so much is at stake when we pray. Still, *patience* as well as persistence is a requirement for prayer. When we are ready to quit, God might be just warming up. When we have decided to classify a prayer as unanswered, God might be just about to answer it.

Authors of classic books on prayer remind us again and again to be patient with God. Harry Emerson Fosdick counsels, "Men often call their petitions unanswered because in their impatience they do not give God time."[5] O. Hallesby adds, "We are too impatient at all times and not least when we pray. This is especially true when there is something urgent, either with us or with someone who is dear to us."[6]

KNOWING REDEMPTIVE HISTORY

God's plan for history is more grandiose than the vision of the most wild-eyed utopian. It dazzles the eyes and boggles the mind. I find that knowing redemptive history enables me to pray with greater insight. It is like having a map to guide you on a long, perilous, exciting journey.

The outline of redemptive history is clear enough. God created the world and called it good. It was beautiful and harmonious and complete. But Adam and Eve rebelled against God. Their rebellion set in motion a chain reaction of evil that tainted everything—humanity's relationship with God, the human community, the natural world, even social institutions. So God set out to restore the world, to fix what was broken, to make all things right again. He initiated his plan of redemption. The main features of the story of redemption are recorded in the Bible.

The redemptive story shows us how to pray. It tells us to be flexible, patient, and above all, visionary. Take the story of Ruth, which occurred around 1100 B.C. Naomi and her husband couldn't make a living in famine-stricken Bethlehem, a small town in Israel, so they decided to move to a foreign country, Moab, then on friendly terms with Israel. There they settled down and built a life for themselves. Their two young sons grew up and married. Naomi assumed that she would remain in Moab, surrounded by her dear family, for the rest of her life.

But her husband died unexpectedly, and then her two sons. Embittered by her fate, she decided to move back to Bethlehem to seek her fortune there. Her prospects in either place were dim. But if she was going to be poor and miserable, she figured she might as well be poor and miserable in her homeland. She forbade her daughters-in-law from traveling with her, knowing that they would stand a better chance of finding husbands if they remained in Moab. One daughter-in-law, Orpah, stayed. The other, Ruth, refused to leave Naomi's side.

So Naomi returned to Bethlehem, accompanied by her loyal daughter-in-law Ruth. By this time Naomi had changed her name to "Mara," which means bitter. She felt utterly hopeless and helpless. She wondered how she could survive without a husband, property, or employment. To stave off starvation, she sent Ruth into the fields to glean grain.

While working in the fields one day, Ruth met Boaz, an older, wealthy man and a relative of Naomi's. He graciously offered Ruth his protection. Eventually Boaz proposed to Ruth, and they were married. It probably wasn't the match that Ruth would have wanted, but it was the match God wanted. In this case, it was a match made literally in heaven. Ruth became pregnant and had a son, who was named Obed. In time Obed married, and his wife had a son, who was named Jesse. Years later, long after Ruth and Naomi had died, Jesse married, and his wife had eight sons. One of them, David, became the king of Israel. But the story wasn't over yet. Centuries later one of Ruth's descendents had a son named Jesus, who became the Savior of the world.

Ruth was a convert to Naomi's religion, the religion of Israel. Like any faithful Israelite, Naomi most likely prayed. Prayer must have seemed like a futile exercise to Naomi, about as effective as wishing upon a star. Naomi and Ruth had to wait much longer than eighteen days to see their prayers answered. The end of the story was happy, to be sure. Naomi got her life back again, Ruth a husband, Boaz a wife, and everyone a baby to oogle over.

Still, that was not the end of the story. It took centuries before the real ending occurred. Ruth had no idea what lay ahead, no awareness of God's plan for the salvation of the world, no knowledge of Jesus, who nevertheless came from the union between Boaz and her. That was how God eventually answered her prayer. The story of Ruth teaches us that when we pray, we must think big, as big as an epic, and use our imagination, keeping our eyes peeled for signs of the strange way God works to redeem the world.

Cotton Mather, Puritan pastor and spiritual writer, argued that we won't see the full impact of our prayers until we get to heaven. We pray by faith now, and often in ignorance. Only God knows how it all fits together.

> When I arrive to the heavenly World, where I shall reap the rich Harvest of all my Devotions here, the Holy Spirit having all my Prayers in a most perfect Remembrance, will then heap in upon me the Answers of them with Blessings of Goodness, far beyond all that I can see or think. Oh! Let the strong Faith of his produce in me a very praying Life, and give Life to my Prayers, and make my sowing Time to be very diligent and plentiful.[7]

If we give God time, he usually does something bigger and better than what we could have imagined, making even fairy tales seem trite and boring.

If we give God time, he usually does something bigger and better than what we could have imagined, making even fairy tales seem trite and boring.

SURPRISING ANSWERS TO PRAYER

In the first chapter I told the stories of people who had been disappointed because God failed to answer their prayers. Their stories—Bob Mitchell's, Pete and Shirley's, Eddie's, and my own—underscored how painful unanswered prayer can be. In each case the results were devastating, at least for awhile anyway.

But not, as it turned out, forever. Bob Mitchell had prayed for the protection of five young missionaries who were trying to make first contact with a remote tribe hidden in the jungles of South America. All five were murdered by members of the tribe. The loss of those five missionaries was catastrophic.

Years later Bob was attending an international conference, held in Europe, for evangelists from around the world. He bumped into an old friend on the elevator, who introduced Bob to an evangelist from South America. In the course of their conversation Bob learned that the evangelist was one of the Auca Indians who had murdered his friend, Jim Eliott, and the four others who were with him. Bob was dumbstruck by the experience, as if he were having an epiphany. His prayer had been mysteriously answered, though not in the way he asked, expected, or wanted. The Auca Indians had become Christians, at least in part because of the death of those five missionaries. The proof was standing right before Bob's eyes.

Pete and Shirley, under some pressure from the leadership of the church, chose to resign from their church just before they were ready to retire because, as their critics charged, the church lacked vision and was not growing fast enough. Though they had fasted and prayed, God did not respond as they had hoped. They thought that God had betrayed and abandoned them.

But their story did not end then and there. God continued to work out his redemptive plan. Pete and Shirley joined Campus Crusade staff, specializing in pastoral care. Crisscrossing Canada and the United States, Pete talked with hundreds of discouraged, weary, and wounded pastors. God began to birth the idea of OASIS RETREATS ministry. Now, over four years later, this retreat ministry provides a safe and restorative place for those in ministry who have been wounded by conflict, betrayal, failure, and loss. Of the hundreds from twenty-nine different denominations who have participated in these OASIS retreats, many have spoken with appreciation about the impact it has had on their personal lives and on their ministries. One commented, "We would not be in ministry today had it not been for OASIS. Thank God for your pain. Without that pain you would have never started OASIS."

Pete and Shirley now say, "God has turned evil into good. He has taken our ashes and made something beautiful out of them. He did answer our prayers. He just had a different answer than we could have ever imagined. And it is good."

Eddie's story continues to unfold. His request for a visa was denied three times. Since then he has joined the staff of a thriving evangelical church in Nairobi. In the past decade that church has planted a dozen satellite churches and started two medical clinics in the slums of Nairobi. Eddie has become an apprentice there. I met the pastor of that church two years ago. In the course of our conversation he said to me, "I see the way pastors function in your culture. You hire them as the official Christian of the church, and then he performs for you Sunday after Sunday. You make him do all the work. I want to help the people in my church to live like Christians. They are as important to God and his work as I am. I want to build disciples."

Perhaps Eddie's prayer to receive the best education is really being answered. He doesn't have to move. He is getting what he needs right there.

I lost one of my children, Diana Jane, in the accident. That experience was devastating. But three of my children survived. Since the accident I have had the privilege of raising them as a single father. I have raised them on my knees. Now, eleven years later, I can say that God has answered my prayers. They are extraordinary human beings—scarred by the accident, to be sure, but also enveloped by grace. They are well on their way to becoming strong Christian leaders. It has been an honor and joy to raise them. God has been good.

God didn't answer our prayers, at least not as we asked them. Bob lost friends to martyrdom, Pete and Shirley lost their church, Eddie lost an opportunity to study in the United States, and I lost three members of my family. Those losses were irreversible, and I refuse to whitewash them. The breadth and depth of pain is all too great. I have no easy, convenient, or rational reasons that explain why these tragedies occurred, nor a magical salve that will bring instant healing to the wounds that remain, even after all these years. Pain is pain, whether or not we fight it, flee from it, or yield to it.

Yet our prayers were answered too, though not in a way any of us could have imagined. That is how prayer seems to work. Rarely does it send an arrow straight to the target; instead, it shoots an arrow that curves and ricochets and even appears to fall short. But in the end it strikes the target, though in ways no one could have predicted or foreseen. Prayer ends up writing an epic, not a short story.

"I WILL SEND YOU"

Prayer is dangerous because God may choose to answer our prayers *through us.* It is impossible to pray as a disinterested, uninvolved party. We are part of the very spiritual ecosystem we live in and pray for. How God answers our prayers may actually require something from us. We might become part of the solution to the problem we are praying about. We might be implicated in the answer we seek. God's redemptive plan will involve us, not bypass us.

Take Moses. He was raised in all the splendor of Egypt. But he could never forget his background. He was a Hebrew and a son of slaves, though he lived in the court of a king. He could never quite figure out where he fit in, which group he belonged to, or what he believed in. One day he wandered away from the court to see his people, the Hebrews, up close. He spied an Egyptian beating a Hebrew slave. Outraged, he killed the Egyptian. When word of his crime leaked out, he had to flee for his life. He crossed a huge desert and eventually found refuge in another land, where he started his life over again. He married, had children, and worked as a shepherd. He found safety and security, or so he thought.

But the Hebrews continued to suffer as slaves, and they cried out to God for deliverance. God heard their prayers and answered them. Meanwhile, Moses had decided to graze his animals close to a mountain that was known as "the mountain of God." Perhaps he wanted to see if the old wives' tales about the place were really true. On that mountain he saw something that awakened his curiosity. A bush was on fire, though it was not being consumed. He decided to investigate.

When he drew near to the sight, he heard a voice from heaven. "Moses! Moses!" Overwhelmed by a sense of dread, he fell on his face before God. God spoke again, informing Moses that he was the same God who had revealed himself to Moses' ancestors, to Abraham, Isaac, and Jacob. He was the God of Moses' past. This God cared about his people, the Hebrews. "I have indeed seen the misery of my people in Egypt. I have heard them crying out because of their slave drivers, and I am concerned about their suffering. So I have come down to rescue them from the hand of the Egyptians. . . ."

But God was not finished yet. He had heard the prayers of his people, identified the problem, and expressed his anger and concern. But he had not yet provided the solution. "So now, go," he said to Moses. "I am sending *you* to Pharaoh to bring my people the Israelites out of Egypt." Suddenly Moses discovered that the God of his past and the God of his people was his God too. God would answer the prayers of his people through him.[8]

Should this surprise us? My study of history reminds me that the people who pray usually end up being the same people who serve, sacrifice, and exercise influence. Perhaps their praying catapulted them into action. Recently I have started to read missionary biographies to learn more about how Western missionaries contributed to the growth of the church around the world in the eighteenth and nineteenth centuries. These biographies, I am discovering, do more than tell a story about missions and missionaries. They also challenge the reader to embrace the vision of these courageous men and women.

One theme keeps surfacing in these books. People like Hudson Taylor, Mary Slessor, Ida Scudder, and C. T. Studd prayed for the salvation of the world. Before long they found themselves traveling to some exotic place to contribute to the very cause that inspired them to pray. They became part of the answer to their own prayers.

Hudson Taylor, founder of the renown China Inland Mission, had to return to England after spending several frustrating and fruitless years in China. These "hidden years," as his son and daughter-in-law called them, seemed to have kept Taylor from fulfilling his missionary dream. He prayed for help and relief, but received nothing of what he asked for. But over time he discovered why. His biographers write of this discovery:

> But the real crisis came when prayer no longer brought relief, but seemed to commit him more and more to the undertaking from which he shrank. For he began to see in the light of that open Book that God could use him, even him, to answer his own prayers.[9]

As I write this book, Jews and Palestinians continue to kill each other in the Middle East. Most Americans have wisely chosen to stay away from Israel, afraid of what could happen if a suicide bomber exploded a bomb right where they just happened to be. But not everyone reacts this way. Marla Bennett, a student at Hebrew University, chose to stay, in spite of the danger. She wrote an essay on her experience that appeared in the *San Diego Jewish Press-Heritage* on May 10, 2002.

Aware of the possibility of death, especially whenever she passed through a public place, Marla chose to remain in Israel because she wanted to be a part of the solution. "At least," she wrote, "if I am here I can take an active role in attempting to put back together all that has broken. I can volunteer in the homes of Israelis affected by terrorism. I can put food in collection baskets for Palestinian families." Though she agreed with the loved ones who urged her to leave, she decided nevertheless to stay. "It is dangerous here. I appreciate their concern. But there is nowhere else in the world I would rather be right now. I have a front-row seat for the history of the Jewish people. I am a part of the struggle for Israel's survival. . . . I know that this struggle is worth it."[10] She died on July 31, 2002, when a Palestinian blew himself up in the middle of the university.

Prayer does more than put us in a front-row seat, as Bennett mentioned. It puts us on stage. We become a player in God's redemptive work because God will somehow use us to answer our own prayers.

There is thus no safety in prayer. Our prayers will thrust us into the action—into relationships, causes, institutions, conflicts, and needs—all of which will demand our time, our resources, even our lives. The answers we pray for will involve us, change us, and redirect the course of our lives. If we pray for peace, we will have to become peacemakers. If we pray for justice, we will be forced to uphold the cause of justice. If we pray for the salvation of the world, we will be given opportunities to share the good news.

Most of our prayers fall short because they are too cautious and conservative. We want problems to disappear but not necessarily be solved; we want symptoms to be treated while the disease continues to progress; we want conflicts to be smoothed over, though the underlying issues remain untouched. We long for convenience and security.

But God thinks bigger than that. He plans to redeem the world, and he will use us in the process. So that is how we must pray.

Those nine miners had to spend eighteen hours in that mine, thinking that the rescue operation had stopped, either because the rescue workers had failed or because they had given up. They had to contend with bad air, cold, wet, darkness, and despair. Amazingly, they continued to hope and pray. They had no idea what was happening above ground, which, as we know, was another story altogether, for the rescue workers were busy around the clock doing everything they could to get the miners out.

Their story is our story. Just so must we pray, with all the boldness and audacity we can muster, however long we have to wait for answers and however weary and broken we feel. For God will answer our prayers, perhaps not how we wanted or when we wanted but in a way that we truly longed for in the depths of our being.

QUESTIONS FOR DISCUSSION

1. Think of some occasions when you had to wait for a long time before your prayers were answered? What was it like to have to wait so long?

2. Can you think of some examples of prayer that were answered in a different way than how you wanted and expected but in a way that was actually better?

3. Why is God's timetable so different from our own? Can waiting ever be good for us? Why?

4. What happens when we begin to pray with God's redemptive plan in mind rather than our personal desires? How will that affect our view of answers to prayer?

5. In what way is prayer a risky business?

6. How might God want to use you to help answer your own prayers?

EPILOGUE

More tears are shed over answered prayer
than unanswered prayer.
MOTHER TERESA

I MENTIONED THE APOSTLE PETER IN THE PROLOGUE. I RETURN TO him now. Peter was brash and bold. He made big promises, but he was not always able to deliver. Just before the crucifixion Peter claimed that he would die with Jesus, even if the other disciples fled. But Jesus challenged his presumption by telling Peter that he would deny him three times. Peter did just that only a few hours later. When accused of being one of Jesus' disciples, Peter buckled under the pressure and swore that he never knew Jesus. He was filled with shame and regret, and he wept bitterly.

But Peter's failure did not have the last word. After the resurrection Jesus restored the relationship. He did it by asking Peter a question. "Simon son of John, do you love me more than these?" Peter replied, "Yes, Lord, you know that I love you." "Feed my lambs," Jesus said. Jesus asked the same question two more times, as if giving Peter a chance to make right what he had done wrong.

It was all too much for Peter. He had just faced his own weakness and vulnerability, and he knew that words alone meant little. As if crying out for help, he said to Jesus, "Lord, you know all things; you know that I love you." Instead of claiming perfect knowledge of himself, he acknowledged that Jesus was the one who had perfect knowledge of him. He realized in that moment that Jesus knew him better than he knew himself. Peter understood that Jesus had the right to ask all the questions and to search the deepest places in Peter's heart. The only thing Peter could say was, "You know everything."

God does know everything, including everything about us. Perhaps that is the true and final answer to the question of unanswered prayer. We might never know why God doesn't answer our prayers. God may seem as distant as eternity, as unfair as evil, and as incomprehensible as infinity. But he is still God—good, powerful, and wise. God is the great initiator, even when we pray. He answers the prayers of the heart because he is the one who put them there in the first place and then called them forth. This poem by Robert Browning sums it up perfectly.

> *If I forget,*
> *Yet God remembers! If these hands of mine*
> *Cease from their clinging, yet the hands divine*
> *Hold me so firmly that I cannot fall;*
> *And sometimes I am too tired to call*
> *For Him to help me, then He reads the prayer*
> *Unspoken in my heart, and lifts my care.*

Eleven years ago I lost Diana Jane. I prayed for her protection that day, but something went wrong. I am no closer now to understanding why she died than I was eleven years ago. It is a terrible and troubling mystery to me.

But I never stopped praying, even in those darkest days after the accident. At first I prayed because it was a habit. Sometimes I wondered why I was praying, though I continued to pray all the same. But now I pray out of deep conviction.

Ironically, I still pray for my children's protection, just as I did before the accident. We don't follow the bedtime ritual we used to.

I figure they are too old for that. They need to learn to pray on their own. Still, we pray together every week as a family. It is not always serious and solemn. Sometimes we end up laughing and fail to get one prayer out of our mouths.

We don't use the prayer we used so many years ago. The kids have outgrown it. It has gone the way of cribs and picture books and flannel pajamas.

> *Now I lay me down to sleep,*
> *I pray thee, Lord, my soul to keep.*
> *If I should die before I wake,*
> *I pray thee, Lord, my soul to take.*

I never thought I would have to take the second half of that prayer seriously. Eleven years ago I did. But not since then. I concentrate on the first half now. I pray that God will keep the souls of my children in his hands and enable them to love God, trust God, and follow God, wherever he leads.

He is answering that prayer.

NOTES

PROLOGUE

1 This translation is from the NRSV.

CHAPTER 1. Are You Listening, God?

1 Armand M. Nicholi Jr., *The Question of God* (New York: Free Press, 2002), 28–29.
2 Barbara Brown Taylor, "Bothering God," *Christian Century* (March 24–31, 1999), 356.
3 Luke 11:9–10.
4 John 14:12–14.
5 Andrew Murray, *With Christ in the School of Prayer* (Old Tappan, N.J.: Spire Books, 1974), 33.
6 Harry Emerson Fosdick, *The Meaning of Prayer* (New York: Association Press, 1915), 40.

CHAPTER 2. The True Heart of Prayer

1 John Calvin, *Golden Booklet of the True Christian Life* (Grand Rapids: Baker, 1952), 53.
2 Luke 18:9.
3 Luke 18:9–14.
4 C. S. Lewis, *Mere Christianity* (New York: Macmillan, 1943), 111.
5 Helmut Thielicke, *The Waiting Father* (San Francisco: Harper & Row, 1959), 133.
6 Helmut Thielicke, *The Waiting Father*, 133.
7 Mark 5:21–24.
8 Mark 5:25–34.
9 Luke 23:39–43.

Chapter 3. Can God Take Our Complaints?

1 Peter De Vries, *The Blood of the Lamb* (Boston: Little, Brown & Company, 1961), 229.
2 Peter De Vries, *The Blood of the Lamb,* 236.
3 John Dillenberger, *John Calvin: Selections from His Writings* (Ann Arbor: Scholars Press, 1971), 23.
4 Psalm 3:1–2.
5 Psalm 6:6–7.
6 Psalm 10:1.
7 Psalm 80:4–5.
8 Psalm 22:14–15.
9 John Chrysostom, *On the Incomprehensible Nature of God* (The Fathers of the Church, vol. 72; Washington: Catholic Univ. Press, 1982), 162.
10 Matthew 26:36–46; Mark 14:32–42; Luke 22:39–46.
11 Psalm 22:1.
12 Psalm 22:1–2, 6–7, 16–17 (NRSV).
13 Psalm 88:13–14.
14 Connie Willis, *Doomsday Book* (New York: Bantam, 1992), 410.
15 Lief Enger, *Peace Like a River* (New York: Grove Press, 2001), 217–18.
16 Psalm 10:1.
17 Psalm 13:1–2.
18 Psalm 38:1–2.
19 Psalm 10:17–18 (NRSV).
20 Psalm 22:19–21.
21 Psalm 22:22–23, 27–28.

Chapter 4. The Gift of Unanswered Prayer

1 Leo Tolstoy, "Prayer," *Divine and Human* (Grand Rapids: Zondervan, 2000), 40.
2 Leo Tolstoy, "Prayer," 41.
3 Leo Tolstoy, "Prayer," 41.
4 J. R. R. Tolkein, *The Fellowship of the Ring: The Lord of the Rings* (New York: Houghton, Mifflin, & Co., 1954), 60.
5 See James 4:4.
6 Philippians 2:6–8.
7 Matthew 26:39.
8 Leo Tolstoy, "Prayer," 42.
9 Hannah Whitall Smith, *The Christian's Secret of a Happy Life* (Old Tappan, N.J.: Spire Books, 1970), 159–60.

CHAPTER 5. Prayer Excavates the Heart

1 Hannah Whitall Smith, *The Christian's Secret of a Happy Life* (Old Tappan, N.J.: Spire Books, 1970), 28.

2 Augustine, *The Confessions* (New York: New City Press, 1997), 198.

3 Augustine, *The Confessions*, 192.

4 Harry Emerson Fosdick, *The Meaning of Prayer* (New York: Association Press, 1915), 133.

5 C. S. Lewis, *The Screwtape Letters* (New York: Macmillan, 1976), 129–32.

6 James 4:2b–3.

7 Luke 7:35–50.

8 Mark 10:46–52.

9 Mark 9:14–29; cf. Luke 9:28–43.

10 Hebrews 11:32–40.

11 John Calvin, *Institutes of the Christian Religion* (Philadelphia: Westminster, 1960), 874.

12 Jean-Pierre de Caussade, *The Sacrament of the Present Moment* (San Francisco: HarperCollins, 1982), 17.

13 Quoted in Henri J. M. Nouwen, *Sabbatical Journey* (New York: Crossroad, 1998), 4.

CHAPTER 6. The Courage to Keep Asking

1 P. T. Forsyth, *The Soul of Prayer* (Vancouver, B.C.: Regent College Publishing, 1997), 16.

2 St. Gregory of Nyssa, *Ascetical Works* (The Fathers of the Church, vol. 58; Washington: Catholic University Press, 1967), 151.

3 Master Geert, "Noteworthy Sayings," *Devotio Moderna: Basic Writings* (Classics of Western Spirituality; Mahwah, N.J.: Paulist, 1988), 76.

4 Luke 18:1–8.

5 Luke 11:5–9.

6 Harry Emerson Fosdick, *The Meaning of Prayer* (New York: Association Press, 1915), 66.

7 John Chrysostom, *On Repentance and Almsgiving* (The Fathers of the Church, vol. 96; Washington: Catholic University Press, 1998), 37.

8 2 Corinthians 12:9–10.

9 Henri Nouwen, *With Open Hands* (New York: Baltimore Books, 1987), 7.

10 Richard Foster, *Celebration of Discipline* (San Francisco: HarperSanFrancisco, 1978), 35.

CHAPTER 7. Praying According to God's Will

1 John 14:13–14.
2 John 15:7.
3 John 16:23–24.
4 This issue of the relationship of the believer to God's will (both revealed and not revealed) is explored in greater detail in my book *Discovering God's Will* (Grand Rapids: Zondervan, 2002).
5 Martin Luther, *Letters of Spiritual Concern* (Library of Christian Classics, vol. 18; Philadelphia: Westminster, 1955).
6 Joseph F. Power, ed., *Francis de Sales: Finding God Wherever You Are* (New York: New City Press, 1993), 110–46.
7 John Calvin, *Institutes of the Christian Religion* (Philadelphia: Westminster, 1960), 850.
8 C. S. Lewis, *Mere Christianity* (New York: Macmillan, 1960), 182.
9 Romans 12:1–2 (emphasis added).
10 2 Corinthians 12:10.
11 Luke 22:42.
12 Philippians 1:9–11.
13 Ephesians 3:16–19.
14 See Psalm 90 and 139.
15 O. Hallesby, *Prayer* (Minneapolis: Augsburg, 1994), 24.
16 Genesis 37–50.
17 Acts 4:27–28.
18 St. Gregory of Nyssa, as quoted in Timothy George, "Is the God of Muhammad the Father of Jesus?" *Christianity Today* (Feb. 4, 2002), 34.
19 Karl Barth, *Prayer* (Philadelphia: Westminster, 1946), 96.
20 P. T. Forsyth, *The Soul of Prayer* (Vancouver, B.C.: Regent College Publishing, 1997), 71.
21 Hans Urs von Balthasar, *Prayer* (San Francisco: Ignatius Press, 1986), 15.
22 Charles E. Moore, *Provocations: Spiritual Writings of Kierkegaard* (Farmington, Pa.: Plough, 1999), 345.

Chapter 8. Prayer Is Not About Us!

1 Excerpt from "August Rain, After Haying," copyright 1996 by the Estate of Jane Kenyon. Reprinted from *Otherwise: New & Selected Poems*, with the permission of Graywolf Press, Saint Paul, Minnesota.

2 Barbara Brown Taylor, "Bothering God," *Christian Century* (March 24–31, 1999), 356.

3 St. Ignatius of Loyola, *The Spiritual Exercises of St. Ignatius* (New York: Doubleday, 1964), 54.

4 Owen Chadwick, *The Conferences of John Cassian: Western Aceticism* (Philadelphia: Westminster, 1986), 226.

5 Henri Nouwen, *With Open Hands* (New York: Balantine Books, 1987), 54.

6 Philippians 1:19–26.

7 C. S. Lewis, *Mere Christianity* (New York: Macmillan, 1943), 54.

8 Quoted in Armand M. Nicholi Jr., *The Question of God* (New York: Free Press, 2002), 106.

9 Job 42:2–6.

10 John 17:1, 4–5.

11 Eugene Peterson, *Answering God* (San Francisco: HarperCollins, 1989), 23.

CHAPTER 9. Prayer Changes Us

1 C. S. Lewis, *The Great Divorce* (New York: Macmillan, 1946), 72.

2 Eugene Peterson, *Answering God* (San Francisco: HarperCollins, 1989), 1.

3 Oswald Chambers, *My Utmost for His Highest* (Grand Rapids: Discovery House, 1992), Aug. 28.

4 Luke 11:13 (emphasis added).

5 John 16:7.

6 Ephesians 5:18–20; cf. Galatians 5:22–23.

7 2 Corinthians 3:17–18; see also Roman 8:29 and 1 John 3:2.

8 Jean-Pierre De Caussade, *The Sacrament of the Present Moment* (San Francisco: HarperCollins, 1982), 101–2.

9 Hannah Whitall Smith, *The Christian's Secret to a Happy Life* (Old Tappan, N.J.: Spire Books, 1970), 39–40.

10 Emerson Fosdick, *The Meaning of Prayer* (New York: Association Press, 1915), 24.

11 Romans 5:3–5.

12 James 1:2–4.

13 Agnieszka Tennant, *Christianity Today* website: www.christianitytoday.com/ct/2002/117/51.0.html.

14 M. Scott Peck, *The Road Less Traveled* (New York: Simon and Schuster, 1978), 15.

15 O. Hallesby, *Prayer* (Minneapolis: Augsburg, 1994), 22.

CHAPTER 10. The Epic Story

1 Dirk Johnson, "Miraculously, 'All Nine Are Alive,'" *Newsweek* (August 5, 2002), 28–29; "As Waters Rose, Pennsylvania Miners Wrote Words of Love," *Spokesman-Review* (July 29, 2002), A8; "This Time, Region Gets Happy Ending," *Spokesman-Review* (July 29, 2002), A8.
2 Charles E. Moore, ed., *Provocations: Spiritual Writings of Kierkegaard* (Farmington, Pa: Plough Publishing, 1999), 349.
3 John Dillenberger, *John Calvin: Selections from His Writings* (Ann Arbor: Scholars Press, 1971), 26.
4 O. Hallesby, *Prayer* (Minneapolis: Augsburg, 1994), 106.
5 Harry Emerson Fosdick, *The Meaning of Prayer* (New York: Association Press, 1915), 119.
6 O. Hallesby, *Prayer,* 51.
7 Cotton Mather, *Diary of Cotton Mather* (1709–1724) (New York: Frederick Ungar), 22:243.
8 Exodus 3:1–10 (emphasis added).
9 Dr. and Mrs. Howard Taylor, *Hudson Taylor's Spiritual Secret* (Chicago: Moody Press, 1989), 110.
10 Marla Bennett, "Front-row seat for Jewish history," editorial in *The Spokesman-Review,* August 6, 2002, Opinion section, page 4.

Discovering God's Will

How to Make Every Decision with Peace and Confidence

Jerry Sittser

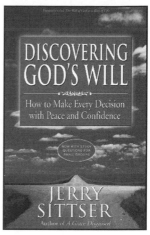

We've all heard that God has a plan for our lives, but what does that mean in practical terms—when we're faced with important life decisions, such as whom to marry, what job to take, where to send our children to school, or what church to join? Sometimes, God's perfect will seems difficult to find, confusing to follow, easy to miss. We may even wonder if we've made past choices that have thrown God's plan for our lives off track.

Discovering God's Will explores important questions like: How free are we if God has a perfect plan for our lives? Does suffering and trouble mean we are off track? How exactly does God speak?

Discussing these and other questions, Jerry Sittser offers a biblically based approach that readers will find truly liberating. No matter what decisions you've already made, he points out that it is still possible to live out God's perfect will for your life—even if you think you've married the wrong person, chosen the wrong career, or landed yourself in some kind of serious trouble.

This new edition includes study questions designed for individual and group use that will be helpful to anyone faced with decisions large and small.

Formerly titled *The Will of God as a Way of Life*

Softcover: 0-310-24600-8

Pick up a copy today at your favorite bookstore!

GRAND RAPIDS, MICHIGAN 49530 USA
WWW.ZONDERVAN.COM

We want to hear from you. Please send your comments about this
book to us in care of zreview@zondervan.com. Thank you.

GRAND RAPIDS, MICHIGAN 49530 USA

WWW.ZONDERVAN.COM